Sir Roger Scruton, who died just after completing this book, was a writer and philosopher who held positions at the universities of London, Oxford, Boston, St Andrews and Buckingham and who wrote widely on art, architecture, music and aesthetics. His books include his now classic *Short History of Modern Philosophy* (1981), *The Aesthetics of Music* (1997), *Death-Devoted Heart: Sex and the Sacred in Wagner's Tristan and Isolde* (2004) and *The Ring of Truth: The Wisdom of Wagner's Ring of the Nibelung* (2016). He was a Fellow of the British Academy and a Fellow of the Royal Society of Literature.

ROGER SCRUTON

Wagner's Parsifal
The Music of Redemption

PENGUIN BOOKS

PENGUIN BOOKS

UK | USA | Canada | Ireland | Australia
India | New Zealand | South Africa

Penguin Books is part of the Penguin Random House group of companies whose addresses
can be found at global.penguinrandomhouse.com.

First published by Allen Lane 2020
Published in Penguin Books 2021
001

Copyright © the Estate of Roger Scruton, 2020

The moral right of the author has been asserted

Printed in Great Britain by Clays Ltd, Elcograf S.p.A.

The authorized representative in the EEA is Penguin Random House Ireland,
Morrison Chambers, 32 Nassau Street, Dublin D02 YH68

A CIP catalogue record for this book is available from the British Library

ISBN: 978-0-141-99166-5

Contents

Publisher's Note

Roger Scruton died just after completing the editorial work on this book, but he was not able to read the proofs or to check the musical examples. The publisher is most grateful to Professor Robin Holloway of Gonville & Caius College, Cambridge for undertaking this task. They also wish to thank Ms. Izzy Larthe for helping them to see the book through the press.

Preface

Wagner steps forward from his works with a belligerent determination to take charge of them, to conduct them into the emotions of his audience and to manage the result. This is particularly true of his last music drama. Blatantly borrowing the holiest of Christian rituals, *Parsifal* invites us to believe in 'the Redeemer'. But it was unclear to many at the time of its first performance whether Wagner had Christ or himself in mind. Commenting on the German Wagner Society's placing of a wreath on the composer's memorial, on which were inscribed the last words of *Parsifal*: 'Redemption to the Redeemer', Nietzsche wrote: 'Many (strangely enough) made the small correction: "Redemption from the Redeemer". One breathed a sigh of relief.'[1]

Nor have things changed since those times. On the contrary, thanks to Wagner's writings and Cosima Wagner's copious diaries, almost nothing of the composer is hidden from us. The temptation is to see all his works as really about Wagner himself, expressions of his real-life obsessions. And, among those obsessions, anti-Semitism, which loomed large in Wagner's life, looms yet larger in the minds of his most determined critics, to the extent that some have seen *Parsifal* as an explicitly anti-Semitic work, a defence of Aryan racial purity against the pollution introduced by the Jews.[2]

Whether or not we agree with that approach, which has become a kind of orthodoxy among critics today, we should recognize the force, in Wagner's life as well as his art, of the ideal of artistic objectivity. The true work of art, Wagner believed, stands above human life in a posture of impartial judgement. The artist is the servant of such a work, duty-bound to express its inner truth in intelligible symbols. Each true work of art is shaped, for Wagner, by its own unifying idea, through which some deep and vital aspect of the human condition achieves imaginative embodiment. The artist's own life is as likely to be an impediment as a stimulus to the creative endeavour, and in any case must be insulated from the creative process.

Of course, an artist draws on his own experience, and might do so with shameless directness, as Dante does in elevating Beatrice to the status of his guide in Paradise. But for the great artist personal experience illustrates an independent and universal meaning, as did Dante's encounter with Beatrice and Wagner's with Mathilde Wesendonck. In both cases the real-life passion was reimagined as something else: something lying beyond the reach of any ordinary human attachment.

Wagner based his mature works in myths and legends, borrowed from the art and religion of medieval times. Far from wishing to hide his own obsessions within the myths, his intention was to extract their core of truth and to present it to his contemporaries, however surprised they might be to discover themselves in this old material. In this way, he believed, art would serve as the successor to religion, a way of acquainting sceptical modern audiences with the truths once made available by faith, including the truth, central to the action of *Parsifal*, that we fall inevitably into guilt and suffering and live with the need to be healed.

The composer described *Parsifal* not as an opera or a music-drama, but as a *Bühnenweihfestspiel*, 'a festival play for the consecration of the stage', so adding one more provocation to the many contained in the body of the work. The drama draws heavily on Christian ritual and symbolism, and somewhat less heavily on Buddhist morality and metaphysics. But the vision of redemption that it outlines is Wagner's answer to a question that concerns us all: the question of how to live in right relation with others, even if there is no God to help us. As several commentators have pointed out,[3] Wagner's anti-Semitism, however crabbed and crazy it became in time, began in hostility towards Judaism as a faith and a culture, and in particular towards the God of the Hebrew Bible. Wagner saw the mission of Jesus as directed against that fierce but capricious deity, on behalf of a love that is rooted in human nature. The abstract judge and law-giver, brought to earth in human form, learned many things, not least self-sacrifice and compassion. And he proved his Godliness not by fire, brimstone and genocides, but by meekly surrendering to the cruellest death that human beings could devise for him. It is this new God, incarnate in Christ, who is invoked throughout *Parsifal* as the Redeemer. Those looking for anti-Semitism will find it in *Parsifal* as they will find it in *The Merchant of Venice* and *The Brothers Karamazov*. But they may also miss the real meaning of Wagner's work, which is that we can be redeemed from our faults, that one included.

Earlier versions of this work were read by Derrick Everett, Jonathan Gaisman, Alicja Gescinska, Paul Heise, Andrew Huddleston, Samuel Hughes and Ian Venables, and I am grateful for their many illuminating comments. I am most of all indebted to four people who have challenged my approach from the basis of their deep understanding of Wagner's difficult and paradoxical work: Andreas Dorschel, Bob Grant, Robin Holloway and Philip Kitcher. My own interpretation, which I put forward here with all diffidence, owes everything to their informed and combative responses. Finally, I owe a debt of thanks to my editor, Stuart Proffitt, who has responded with suggestions and corrections that have greatly improved my argument.

Scrutopia, August 2019

A Note on Musical Examples

As with the other mature works of Wagner, it is normal for commentators to isolate specific themes, sequences and blocks of musical material as leitmotifs, whenever they play a consistent and recurring role in the musical tapestry. I have gathered what I think to be the principal leitmotifs in Chapter 6, assigning numbers and sometimes names. In the preceding chapter I also give a relatively informal account of the way in which these leitmotifs are used to weave the musical fabric into a continuous whole. My hope is nevertheless that the arguments of Chapters 1–4 can be understood even by those who have only a passing acquaintance with musical notation.

I

The Quest

Parsifal tells the story of a simpleton, who wanders the world in a condition of ignorance, but who eventually rescues a derelict religious community from the woes that have afflicted it. He achieves this feat through sympathy and compassion, but with only a retrospective understanding of what he is doing. Packed into this story is a mesh of psychological symbols, as well as a unique moral philosophy in which compassion is presented as the sole but sufficient answer to our suffering and the key to the meaning of our world. My purpose in writing this book is to clarify that philosophy, by tracing it through the words, the narrative and the music of this great but puzzling masterpiece.

The action begins when the boy Parsifal, armed with a homemade bow and arrow, stumbles into Monsalvat, the castle of the Grail knights, guardians of the holy chalice in which Christ's blood was collected at the Crucifixion. The wise knight Gurnemanz, appalled by the boy's shooting of a swan, decides to take him in hand. He teaches him that animals suffer and demand our compassion, and calms Parsifal's rage when the boy learns from Kundry, the dishevelled woman who serves the knights of the Grail, that his mother has, in his absence, died of grief. Gurnemanz then takes Parsifal to the temple of the Grail. There, witnessing the wounded Grail king Amfortas, whose duty in serving the Eucharist causes him excruciating pain, Parsifal is struck dumb with pity. A prophecy, spoken as though from the Grail, had told of *der reine Tor, durch Mitleid wissend* – the pure fool, 'knowing through compassion' – who will rescue the community and its wounded king. But the speechless visitor seems totally inadequate to the role, and Gurnemanz, having at first thought this might be the saviour, impatiently pushes him from the temple.

I

Parsifal resumes his wanderings, and is drawn by a spell to the enchanted castle of Klingsor, the knight turned wizard who, in his desire to seize the Grail, has devoted his magic powers to enticing the knights away from their religious duty into a garden of delight, where flower-maidens offer sexual pleasure. Klingsor is immune to this pleasure, having castrated himself in the hope of achieving the chastity that will bring him within reach of the Grail. But this unholy self-mutilation, through which he has obtained magic powers, has also led to his expulsion from Monsalvat by Titurel, Amfortas's father and the founder of the knightly order. Klingsor now seeks revenge. By tempting the Grail knights he hopes to destroy the order of the Grail, and to take possession of the holy vessel.

Amfortas's pain is alleviated from time to time by salves, which Kundry, journeying in mysterious ways, obtains from distant lands. When he first received the Grail, and set out to build the castle of Monsalvat as its sanctuary, Titurel had discovered Kundry lying in the undergrowth. Now she serves the Grail knights, riding through the air with their messages, but rebutting all questions with a chilling laugh. For Kundry, as she later reveals, has a secret. In a former life she had mocked the Redeemer in his suffering and sorrow, and for this was condemned to wander the earth in successive reincarnations, a demonic seductress with whom no man is safe. Klingsor has bound her with a spell whereby he can call her to him at any time. Only if she can find the chaste man who resists her, and only if the Redeemer's eyes can again be turned on her in a look of forgiveness, can Kundry be freed from this curse. Until granted those two blessings she is in Klingsor's power, and his devilish control has reduced her to a kind of sex-slave, full of hatred for the tyrant whom she is forced to obey.

When Amfortas had inherited the Grail order from Titurel, he had sought out the castle of Klingsor in order to destroy it, carrying with him for this purpose the sacred Spear, Companion to the Grail. However, it was not Klingsor but Kundry – in her other character as a supremely beautiful young woman – who met him. Falling under her spell Amfortas gave way to her embraces, enabling Klingsor to capture the Spear, the mystical power of which now draws the knights of the Grail to his castle. Amfortas was rescued by his knights, but not before Klingsor had used the captured Spear to implant a wound that resists all healing. Kundry is now to be used again, to turn Parsifal away from his mission, so as to be wounded in his turn.

Forcing his way into the enchanted castle, defeating the enfeebled knights who have been entrapped there and brushing away the flower-maidens who now flutter around him, competing for his favours, Parsifal comes at last to Kundry. In her journeys Kundry has learned many things. She knows Parsifal's name, the name with which his mother, Herzeleide ('heart's grief'), had once addressed him as a child, but thereafter did not use, and she summons him now by means of it. She has learned of Herzeleide's love for Gamuret, the father whom Parsifal never knew, of Herzeleide's lonely death and of the longing and guilt that surround the thought of her in the hero's unexamined soul. She conjures all that Parsifal has lacked in his womanless life and offers it to him in a kiss, his mother's last greeting to her vanished son, and his first kiss of love.

The kiss causes torment; guilt wrestles with desire in Parsifal, and in Kundry too, as she pours out her anguished story, vainly attempting both to give herself entirely and also to be forgiven and healed. Compassion triumphs over desire, as Parsifal recalls Amfortas, the wound and the true cause of the Grail king's unbearable pain, which is the torment of erotic love. He pushes Kundry away, seizes the Spear thrown at him by Klingsor and uses it to make the sign of the cross, so waving the enchanted castle to oblivion, having first asked Kundry how he might find his way back to Monsalvat. She will not tell him, but instead curses the attempt, condemning him once again to wander. 'You know where you can find me,' he says as he leaves on his journey.

Those who come to Monsalvat are brought there by the Grail. After many trials, by which Kundry's curse is in some way extinguished, Parsifal too is brought to Monsalvat, to be greeted by the now seriously aged Gurnemanz, who joyfully recognizes the longed-for Spear, carried by the fool whom he had once pushed from the temple. The old knight explains the meaning of this holy day, Good Friday, in which nature glows with the spirit of renewal, refreshed by the tears of repentant sinners. The contrast between chaste love and erotic passion is reflected in the Good Friday vision of a smiling meadow, superseding the memory of Klingsor's now withered hothouse flowers. Kundry, whom Gurnemanz has found in the bushes and reawoken from what seemed like a profound winter sleep, acknowledges Parsifal as the one who can undo the curse that binds her. Tears of contrition for the first time replace her demonic laughter, and she washes Parsifal's feet in an act of penitence. He baptizes her, so fulfilling her deepest desire, which is to die forgiven by the Redeemer whom once she mocked.

We learn that the order of the Grail is in disarray: Amfortas, unable to bear the pain from his wound, which opens whenever the Grail is unveiled for the communion, has refused to allow the holy vessel to be revealed. Titurel, previously kept alive by the sight of the Grail, has finally died; the knights are wandering on ventures of their own, and the 'love-feast', in which the bread and wine provided by the Grail are enjoyed in communion, no longer occurs. The remaining knights live by foraging, and now, on this Good Friday, Amfortas has agreed to serve communion for the last time, as part of Titurel's obsequies. Gurnemanz leads Parsifal and Kundry to the temple, but Amfortas, called upon to uncover the Grail, again refuses, challenging the knights to kill him instead. Parsifal steps forward to heal the wound, by touching it with the sacred Spear. Kundry, released from her curse and now included in the communion, can die at last, as Parsifal presides as king over the Eucharistic ceremony. A dove hovers above his head, while the choir of knights and pages invoke 'redemption to the Redeemer'.

Presented in Wagner's emotionally saturated way the story might be dismissed as a farrago of nonsense. But it has an ancient and respectable lineage, and Wagner is by no means the first to have searched in the legend of Parsifal for a deeper psychological and religious meaning. He took the main outlines from Wolfram von Eschenbach's *Parzifal*, an extended thirteenth-century romance in vigorous narrative verse, which mixes the tale of Parzifal with that of Gahmuret, his father, and Gawan, his relative at the Court of King Arthur. In Wolfram's narrative knights are constantly risking their lives to win favours from the ladies whom they admire, and jousts occur with the same frequency and to the same effect as car-chases in a B-movie. But Parzifal stands out from the other characters in ways that explain why Wagner was gripped by his story. Parzifal's mother,

4

the Queen Herzeloyde, had been widowed on account of her husband's passion for knighthood and the life of adventure that it entails. She had therefore brought up Parzifal in the forest, ignorant of the ways of the world, and of the ambitions that might cause him to follow his father into the fray. Because of this, and because of an accidental encounter with a troop of knights, Parzifal exists in a state of uncertainty, or *zwîvel*, wanting to belong to the world of action and adventure but not sure how to behave or what to admire in it, not sure even who God is or where He can be found. He takes advice from older knights, and is eventually, after many adventures, treated to a long Good Friday sermon from the hermit Trevrizent, so recognizing his faults and the need for forgiveness.

One of his faults concerns the Grail. In his earlier adventures he had come across the mysterious castle of Munsalvaesche, the castle of the Grail, where he encountered the wounded king, Anfortas. In his naivety he had failed to ask the question that sympathy demands; as a result he must wander in search of the Grail, which can be found only by those whom the Grail itself has summoned. In Wolfram the Grail is a stone, brought from Heaven in the time of the warring angels, which confers its bounty in the form of meat and drink to its community of guardians. In earlier epics it had been a cup or (with Chrétien de Troyes) a salver for the host. Subsequent epics identified it with the chalice of the Last Supper, used by Joseph of Arimathea to collect the blood of Christ as he was brought down from the cross, and thereafter associated with the lance that pierced Christ's side.

Parzifal's quest for the Grail is animated by guilt. He seeks forgiveness for his three great sins: his mother's death from grief when he left home in search of adventure; his crime in killing the Red Knight, his kinsman, whose armour he had subsequently worn; his failure to ask the crucial question of Anfortas, the question ('What ails you?') that would show sympathy for his ruined host.

The Perceval/Parzifal legend, first given by Chrétien de Troyes, whose unfinished epic in French served as Wolfram's model, was subsequently taken up by many medieval poets, French, German, Welsh and English, wound together with the Celtic tales of King Arthur and the Knights of the Round Table, and adapted to Christian usage, being steadily purged of erotic adventures, to become a narrative of the chaste knight who rescues ladies in distress but only as part of the larger task of rescuing the Christian religion. The quest for the Grail gave rise to a distinct body of medieval French literature, known as the Lancelot Vulgate, in which the quest became a symbol of the hunger for salvation that burns in us all. Already in Wolfram the knights of the Grail are conceived on the model of the Knights Templar, members of a crusading order, bound by vows of poverty, chastity and obedience, and dedicated to the defence of the Temple of the Holy Sepulchre in Jerusalem and of the Christian pilgrims who visit it. In one version the Grail has fallen into pagan hands, and the quest is to rescue it – a version inspired by the First Crusade, and the founding of the Order of Knights Templar in its wake.

In all versions there is an attempt to see through the outward show of chivalry to the inner solitude of a particular knight, whose quest leads to self-knowledge as his ordeals accumulate. As with the Tristan whom he conjured from Gottfried von Strassburg's *Tristan und Isôt*, Wagner saw in Wolfram's Parzifal the premonition of a spiritual condition that would come fully to fruition only in modern times, when the grip of old customs and static communities had made room for the self-defining individual who is searching for meaning in the world as it is. In *Parsifal* Wagner provides his final vision of what redemption means, in a world where it is not God but human beings who provide it. We long for redemption and strive to obtain it; but repentance and contrition are not enough. Redemption comes from the other, who suffers as we suffer, and who, through compassion, offers to share our burden, and to retrieve what we have lost.

At the heart of the Grail legend is a paradox. We sinners, burdened by guilt, search the world for the trace left by the one who came to redeem us. We find this trace, the Holy Grail, only when called to it. We then discover that it is not we but the Grail that must be rescued. The kingdom of the Grail – the kingdom that Christ came to establish – is in a state of grief and lamentation. The one who seeks salvation must rescue the haven that was to provide it. The religion of the Saviour must itself be saved. That paradox is present at every point in Wagner's narrative. It is contained in the final words of Wagner's drama – 'redemption to the Redeemer' – at which point it has not been solved, but simply displayed in all its aspects. It is the primal

6

mystery which, like the serpent Kundalini, lies coiled in the heart of Being.

Before sketching his first ideas for *Parsifal* in 1857, Wagner had developed another motif from Wolfram's epic, which he had read on a health cure in Marienbad in 1845. In the concluding lines of his poem Wolfram invokes the kingdom of the Grail, whose knights remain both detached from ordinary events and ready to intervene in them, appearing incognito in pursuit of the good deeds commanded by the Grail. One such knight, Loherangrin, Parzifal's son, is called to a princess of Brabant, who has vowed to marry only the man sent to her by God, and as a result has incurred the wrath of the local nobles, to whom she has denied all hope of the crown. Loherangrin is brought to Antwerp by a swan, to offer himself to the princess, on condition that she should refrain from enquiring into his origin and name, a condition that she finally violates, so losing her husband.

This story – a mere hint at the end of Wolfram's poem, though developed in other medieval epics, notably in the thirteenth-century *Lohengrin* by Nouhusius – became, in Wagner's hands, an operatic masterpiece. *Lohengrin*, first performed in 1850, centres on two characters governed by sexual fantasy. Elsa of Brabant, target of jealousy and revenge, clings to the fantasy of the knight in shining armour who will come to her rescue. Lohengrin, the love-struck knight of the Grail, clings to the fantasy that he can enjoy Elsa but not be possessed by her, so that what he is in himself might remain always in that other place, the sacred sphere of belonging where no woman can really capture him. Those two fantasies, known in one form or another to all of us, are used by Wagner to create a gripping and tragic narrative in which the Grail symbolizes the apartness from the worldly order of the true knight, who can offer sexual love only precariously, and on a condition that no normal woman can obey, and no normal man would inflict on her.

If there were nothing more to *Lohengrin* than an elaborate fairy story then of course we should not give it the attention that it claims. In Wagner, however, the raw material of sexual feeling is shaped by character and plot, as well as by the sublime music, and is used to show earthly passion wrestling with spiritual ideals. Wagner adapts the old Flemish story of the swan-knight so as to convey real insights into what is both inescapable and noble in the human condition. The touching innocence of Elsa, the evil machinations of Ortrud, and the stiff chivalry of Lohengrin are all believable, both as archetypes and as individual character-portraits. The familiar fairy-tale device of the question that must not be asked becomes, in Wagner's hands, an instrument to probe the deeper reaches of human frailty, revealing the precariousness even of the most devoted love. And glimpsed throughout the drama is the distant vision of the Grail.

Everything that occurs is bathed in the light from that source, home of our ideals, which exists over the horizon of our searching, but which can never be reached unless it chooses to make itself present before us. It is to this idea, incomparably invoked in the Prelude to Act I of *Lohengrin*, that Wagner returns in *Parsifal*, but with a deepened sense of what it means. The sanctuary of the Grail, as presented in *Parsifal*, is no longer the haven of peace and holiness that was intended when the gift was brought down to us; it has been desecrated, so as to become a place of suffering and lamentation. Those who seek the Grail may stumble into the sanctuary at any time. But they will know that they have arrived there only from what it asks of them, not from what it offers. It is the summons to compassion, in a world of suffering and sin.

Magic and miracles abound in the Grail literature, but they do not carry a burden of meaning in any way comparable to the burden that they bear in Wagner's last opera. *Parsifal* presents the symbols and rites of the Christian religion as objects of emotion in themselves, detached from the theology that underpins them. Some recent commentators, notably Lucy Beckett, conceive the drama as a Christian work of art, perhaps not as Christian as the *Divine Comedy* of Dante, but at any rate Christian in the personal and questioning manner of Milton's *Paradise Lost*.[1] Others, Ulrike Kienzle most persuasively, rewrite the Christian symbolism in terms of the Schopenhauerian philosophy that dominated Wagner's thinking in his later years.[2] Others still assimilate the symbols, and the Grail legend in all its versions, to the 'archetypes' of Jungian psychology, setting the religion aside and rehearsing instead the story of the Mother, as portrayed and preserved in the unconscious of us all. Such is Joseph Campbell, in his influential *summa mythologica*, one long section of which runs

Wolfram's *Parzifal*, Wagner's *Parsifal* and James Joyce's *Ulysses* and *Finnegans Wake* together as exhalations of the 'Paraclete' (the advocate or helper, identified in Christian theology with the Holy Ghost).[3] Yet others attack the opera precisely for its Christian allusions, even suggesting, with Nietzsche, that they are used to claim far-reaching significance for emotions that are in themselves merely life-denying. 'I despise everyone,' Nietzsche wrote, 'who does not experience *Parsifal* as an attempted assassination of basic ethics.'[4]

The protagonists of *Parsifal* are heirs to religious doctrines, and are amply supplied with the miracles that will reinforce their belief in them. It does not follow that Wagner is committed to the *truth* of those doctrines. The drama would be pointless if it did not take the beliefs of the characters seriously, or put those beliefs to the kind of *moral*, rather than intellectual, test that is the real substance of a drama. At the same time, Wagner does not stand at a distance from the worldview of his characters. He does not look on the Christian faith with irony, or dismiss it as a posture that we can no longer share. On the contrary, he looks in it for signs of what is deep in all of us, and for what might be revealed and hallowed through its artistic expression. In a celebrated essay on 'Religion and Art', published in 1880 during preparations for the first performance of *Parsifal* in Bayreuth, Wagner wrote that 'it is reserved to art to salvage the kernel of religion, inasmuch as the mythical images which religion would wish to be believed as true are apprehended in art for their symbolic value, and through ideal representation of those symbols art reveals the concealed deep truth within them.'[5]

It is abundantly clear from Wagner's life and writings that he was not a Christian believer, and in his early correspondence with Liszt he vigorously resists his future father-in-law's attempts to bring him into the fold of the Catholic Church. His stance throughout life was that expressed to Cosima: 'I do not believe in God; but I believe in godliness.'[6] Quite what is meant by 'godliness' (*Göttlichkeit*), when there is no God to provide it, is one of the many questions posed by the drama. 'Godliness', in Wagner's thinking, is the 'concealed deep truth' within the religious symbols of *Parsifal*. Through godliness we both rescue each other from degradation and also re-consecrate our lives. In *Parsifal* this godliness wears Christian costumes, up to a point. The hallowed objects, rites and persons of the Christian faith are part of what is happening, 'real presences' in the psyche of the protagonists, like the gods in Greek tragedy. The Eucharistic ceremony is represented on the stage; but in a sense it is also performed there, since nothing is lacking other than the priesthood of the one who sings the part of Amfortas. The Redeemer who dies on the cross, the penitent Magdalene, the sacraments of baptism and Holy Communion, the vow of celibacy, the Grail and lance as interpreted by medieval iconography, the mystery of Good Friday, not to speak of the doctrines of sin, repentance and atonement implied in the whole sublime and sacred story of Christ's life – all these are represented in the drama.

The conjured scene departs from the Christian worldview, however, in ways that are critical to the drama's meaning. For instance, the creator God is invoked only in passing, and never as an object of worship or prayer. Much is said about the Redeemer, but nothing about the place whence he came or the place to which he has departed. The ritual, superficially so very like Holy Communion, emphasizes courage, action and renewal, rather than (as in the Church's litany) sin, confession, repentance and redemption. The Magdalene figure, Kundry, is a symbol of contrition only in one half of her being; in the other half she is a demonic distillation of sexual allure. She is also the latest of many reincarnations by which she belongs both to the life of Parsifal and to the life of Christ.

This last point is significant. When Wagner first had the idea for *Parsifal* it was in the wake of his reading of Schopenhauer in 1854, when he also conceived both *Tristan und Isolde* and the Buddhist opera (never composed) *The Victors*. Schopenhauer was an atheist, who nevertheless had great respect for Indian religions and for Buddhism in particular.[7] He also admired the person of Christ, and the Christian ethic of compassion. The Hindu idea of reincarnation symbolized for Schopenhauer the restless striving of the will, from one embodiment to another, always in error, and never brought to quietus. Wagner, like Schopenhauer, believed that the deep truth of Christianity coincides with that of Buddhism, and that the doctrine of reincarnation corresponds to a crucial element in both religions: the belief that sin endures until erased by contrition and forgiveness.

For Schopenhauer sin is the mistake of existing as an individual, while salvation means rectifying that mistake, through the renunciation of the will.[8] Exploited dramatically, in the character of Kundry, those ideas symbolize both the hounding of the sinner by her sin, and the sundering of the personality under the impact of a guilt that has not met with forgiveness – neither forgiveness from the other, nor forgiveness from the self. The story of Kundry also typifies Wagner's use of magic – not to promote a belief or to heighten a drama, but to dramatize a real human predicament, in this case to offer a profound and riveting picture of a woman tormented by her sexuality, both longing for purity and doomed to destroy it, who has fallen into the power of a perverted tyrant.

One of the striking features of Wolfram's narrative is that, while ostensibly about individual men and women attached to definite courts and cities, the crucial encounters happen nowhere. People meet unexpectedly in woods or pathways; knights ride towards each other out of misty distances, lance at the ready; ladies are found by the wayside, lamenting calamities that are beyond all help. Parzival is set on his wandering life by a chance encounter with a group of knights, riding from nowhere to nowhere in the forest. The most important place in the story, Munsalvaesche, the castle of the Grail, is likewise found by accident and then promptly lost again.[9] Even to look for it is impossible, since the Grail is revealed only to the one whom the Grail itself has chosen. The holy stone was brought down from Heaven by angels, and the stone remains apart from the world, in an illuminated space of its own. As though in compensation for this 'nowhere' quality Wolfram litters his narrative with the names of people and places – more names per line than in any comparable document – showing an astonishing familiarity with Europe, Scandinavia, Great Britain and the Middle East, and yet ensuring that his readers could never use his poem as a guidebook, should they set out in quest of the Grail.

This nowhere quality of the action is seized upon by Wagner and given powerful dramatic force. Dramas that seem to happen nowhere in fact happen everywhere. They are rooted in universal truths, and the more remote and mythical the setting, the more immediately do they touch on our life. Parsifal appears in Monsalvat without an explanation. The castle is ostensibly separated by a valley or two from the enchanted castle of Klingsor, at a time when the Christian and 'heathen' (i.e. Muslim) worlds were face to face in northern Spain. But the story makes nothing of this, and retains the crucial feature of Wolfram's narrative, which is that the Grail is not of this world, and that there are no directions for finding it. The same is true of the castle of Klingsor, loosely based on Clinschor's Schastel Marveil, where Wolfram's hero, Gawan, undergoes the trials that enable him to liberate the knights and ladies who are enchanted there. Klingsor's castle appears as though conjured from nothing, its girl-flowers creatures of erotic dreams, who could never step from their enchanted garden into the real human world. When Parsifal detaches himself from his seductress and waves the castle away with the recovered Spear, only Kundry remains, a placeless, timeless creature whose real longing is not for Parsifal's embraces here and now, but for the look of pitying forgiveness that was offered in another place and another time – the look of love that she scorned.

Kundry, in her other character as the penitent Magdalene, roams in search of balsam in distant lands, from whence she arrives at Monsalvat in Act I, riding through the air on her witch's mare. She departs again, but in a swoon from which she will awaken in another no-place, where the dark side of her sundered self habitually submits to the wizard who enslaves her. She is the bridge between two imaginary worlds, both rooted in sexual emotion, in one place transcended, in the other exploited and enjoyed. In the search for salvation Parsifal must enter these two worlds, restoring purity and healing to the one only by passing through the delights and torments of the other.

Two profound transformation scenes portray the nowhere character of Monsalvat. The music here, filled with sorrow and yearning, accompanies a change of scene that is less a change than a procession, the whole set moving before the audience's eyes as though composed not of matter, but of thought. ('You see, my son,' sings Gurnemanz, 'that here time becomes space', a line that Wagner repeats to Cosima.)[10] Parsifal is lifted up by the processional music, translated into a spiritual version of himself, in order to participate in a ritual which, like the Grail itself, occurs nowhere and anywhere.

The Greeks made a distinction between two conceptions of time, which they named *chronos* and *kairos*. The first is time in its regular character, measured by the moments as they tick away. *Kairos* time is not measured in that way: it is composed of cruxes, of which, in subsequent Christian thinking, the cross (crux) became the paradigm. At these cruxes the world takes a new turn: the arrow finds its target, the shuttle leaves the hand, the kiss touches the cheek. *Chronos* time is drawn like a veil over a great abyss, in the bottom of which huge landscapes are dimly perceivable. At the *kairos* moments the veil is lifted and another dimension of being is revealed to us. All true myths are attempts to narrate human life as though it takes place in *kairos* time rather than *chronos* time, and religions strive to represent our world of successive moments as the 'moving image of eternity', to use Plato's famous expression in the *Timaeus*. *Parsifal* likewise is a drama of *kairos* time, and this is the true meaning of Gurnemanz's words to Parsifal as they journey to the temple of the Grail.

It is a perennial theme of religion that our sequential, linear experience of time conceals another and deeper awareness, in which time is not linear but circular, and in which the eternal return allows us to peer through the moment to a timeless reality beyond.[11] This awareness cannot be easily described except in clichés; but its inner reality can be expressed, as in the late quartets of Beethoven, and also in the great poem that they inspired, the *Four Quartets* of T. S. Eliot. *Parsifal* belongs with such works. It attempts to dramatize our metaphysical predicament, as prisoners of time whose thoughts are turned towards the timeless. That is why ritual has such an important place in Wagner's drama, as it has in every enduring religion. A ritual takes place at a moment in time: but the event neither begins nor ends with its ritual presentation. We say that it exists eternally, that it recurs for ever, that it lies 'outside time and change' – all metaphors for what cannot be literally described, which is another and deeper awareness of the world, in which the moment is dissolved in its meaning.

Things come into being and pass away, but we find it difficult to accept this fact. In all places and epochs people have believed that there is a door out of time into a place where nothing changes and all is at rest within its being. And the key to this door is repetition: the use of time as a *denial* of change, rather than the locus of change. That is what sacred rituals provide: the prayers, chants, costumes, steps and gestures that must be repeated exactly, and for which there is no explanation other than that this is how it is done, has always been done and will be done for ever.

In Christianity, however, the central ritual gathers us into a larger project, which is the project of our salvation. Christ's sublime offering of himself at the Last Supper was (to use Eliot's words) a 'point of intersection of the timeless with time', a moment in the eternal present, that is not just represented but re-enacted in the ritual of Holy Communion. Christ told us that 'where two or three gather together in my name, there am I with them' (Matthew 18:20), so defining both an item of faith, and a way of understanding the Christian ritual. The ritual repeats the original gift (the sacrifice of the Redeemer) and the original invitation to live in another way. Exactly what the gift amounts to and what we must do to receive it are the points at issue throughout Wagner's opera. The Eucharistic ritual, as Wagner presents it, is a moment of purification and renewal, which reconnects the communicants to what they most deeply wish to be. But the religion of Monsalvat is not based in a promise of another world. It is an invitation to live differently in *this* world, and so to find redemption through our own efforts, and without the help of a God.

Dieter Borchmeyer draws attention to Wagner's reading of August Friedrich Gfrörer's *History of Early Christianity*, 1838, which comes close to interpreting the Christian religion as an 'intransitive' faith, in Erich Heller's sense – a faith that does not point to a life beyond this world, but to another way of living now.[12] It is clear from Cosima's diaries that Wagner was very much of Gfrörer's mind, believing that redemption lies *in* the religious way of life and does not come when life as we know it is over. This is symbolized by the communion ceremony, the moment when the wandering and wounded soul is reincorporated and the life of self-giving is renewed. The heart of the Monsalvat religion is an original sacrifice, which is constantly re-enacted, so as to place it at the centre of the collective consciousness. It is this act of communal renewal that has been polluted, and it is not heresy or any other deviation from a system of belief that has afflicted the kingdom of the Grail, but a wound to the sacred ritual, which is also a wound to its king.

But why is the ritual needed? And why does the sinner have to participate in the Eucharistic ceremony time and again, and with no new thing achieved, but only the old thing, leaving all to be repeated? Whence comes the yearning for another and more ritualized kind of fellowship? What was achieved by the Redeemer whose sacrifice we re-enact in ritual form, and why did he have to suffer? In the world of deals and transactions none of this makes sense. What is at stake in religion, at least religion of the sacramental variety that is the subject of Wagner's drama, is clearly something beyond cost and benefit. Religious people experience a depth of longing and a joy of consolation that bear witness to this, whatever the doctrines of their faith.

Wagner saw the religious way of life not as a bargain between the believer and an all-powerful God, but as a continuous act of self-sacrifice, a dissolving of the self in the experience of community. On this view religious ritual is not something performed for a benefit, but a command to which we submit, in order to exhibit an existential tie. There is a temptation to rewrite human relations in the language of deals, and indeed this is one legacy of the Enlightenment, which aimed to replace hierarchies and inherited authorities with freely chosen laws. Taken to its extreme the 'social contract' vision points to the 'commodification' of human relations, and in his mature operas Wagner showed an acute awareness of this. Human relations could become defeasible and renegotiable as in a market. In the world of markets existential ties, which change the nature and condition of those whom they join, would be increasingly eroded as the contractual worldview expands. All would become a matter of free choice among options, undertaken by self-contained and autonomous individuals within a legally established framework, itself no more than a summary of human agreements.

To a recognizable extent this transition has occurred, since its possibility lies in the human condition itself. Even the most solemn of our obligations will wear away under the impact of instrumental ways of reasoning. The question *cui bono?* – what's the good of it? – is a permanent threat to our commitments. And in many of its versions Christianity has reconciled itself to the 'marketized' view of the human condition, re-describing it in cost/benefit terms, as a deal between God and *Homo economicus*. Original sin brought death into the world; but Christ has stepped in to foot the bill, so we will not die. In the words of St Paul: 'The wages of sin is death; but the gift of God is eternal life through Jesus Christ our Lord' (Romans 6:23). Out of that thought there has emerged over time a kind of religion – a 'vast, moth-eaten, musical brocade / Created to pretend we never die', as Philip Larkin put it. But it is emphatically not the religion envisaged by Wagner, and not religion as we observe it in the wider history of mankind.

Existential ties are a fundamental part of traditional communities, even if they are not so familiar today. In the traditional Christian vow of marriage, for example, two people give themselves to each other, for better or for worse, for the remainder of their lives. They create what Hegel calls a 'substantial' union, one that cannot be transferred from the parties, and whose terms can never be stated or finally fulfilled.[13] The couple root themselves in each other, and their obligations, as a result, become both indefinite and non-transferable. A contract of cohabitation has terms which, when fulfilled, bring the contract to an end; it can be ended by agreement, and its obligations can be transferred by consent. None of that is true of a vow of marriage.

In the distinction between vows and contracts we see one aspect of the deeper distinction between existential and accidental ties. By undertaking a vow people cross a threshold, and traditional societies mark this fact with a rite of passage. Such a rite reflects a society-wide interest in cementing our existential ties. It is a way of incorporating the present members of society into arrangements that are permanent, non-transferable and timeless. That is part of what is meant by calling rituals 'sacraments': they transform a contingent fellowship into a sacred tie, and call down on the community the watchful blessing of its gods. And they do this even when the gods have been reduced, as in Wagner's Eucharist, to a Redeemer who once gave himself as a sacrificial victim, but who has vanished as a result, to exist only in the bread and wine that recall his original sacrifice.

The doctrine of 'transubstantiation' has given force to the belief in Christ's 'real presence' at the altar, and to the conception of the communion as a dialogue with an eternally existing deity. But in Wagner's drama that doctrine is reduced to a metaphor. The 'love-feast' celebrated at Monsalvat is about solidarity here and now, not life beyond the grave, and the most striking feature of the Redeemer is not his real presence at the altar, but his real absence from the lives of those who call to him, as Amfortas calls to him in vain.

How can a community arrive at such a crisis as that represented in Act I of *Parsifal*, in which the ritual that defines and renews its existential ties must be performed, whatever the cost to the individual charged with conducting it? There must be another hunger that is being invoked and assuaged here, beyond the hunger for bread and wine. Underlying the 'love-feast' therefore is a deeper drama, which is the real theme of Wagner's opera. This drama is present in the music, and in the heart of the spectator; but nobody to my knowledge has yet put it into words.

Associated with the world of contracts and deals is the liberal individualist picture of society, as a network of agreements between people, protected by their rights, who freely commit to each other and as freely dissolve their commitments when the job is done. Vows and self-giving are neither necessary nor wise, in a society of free exchange. Give your consent, by all means; but never give yourself. Religion, in such an arrangement, is a marginal affair, a kind of insurance policy designed to protect the individual when things go wrong.

Liberal individualism is an attractive philosophy, and has produced beautiful and influential theories of political legitimacy, including those of Locke, Harrison, Montesquieu, Rousseau and, in our time, John Rawls. But it does not describe real human beings. What matters to us, far more than our deals and bargains, are the ties that we never contracted, that we stumbled into through passion and temptation, as well as the ties that could never be chosen, like those that bind us to our parents, our country, and our religious and cultural inheritance. These ties put us, regardless of our aims and desires, in existential predicaments that we cannot always rectify. Thus it is with the tie to the mother, for example, which forms the background to the drama of *Parsifal*: a tie that gives rise to heartbroken longing and guilt, and which calls upon us at every moment of our lives to honour it.

There are existential ties that are calculated to fulfil us and to complete our being: such is marriage, as traditionally conceived, and such for the knights of the Grail is the vow of celibacy that ties them to the community. But there are ties that bring shame, self-disgust and the sense of pollution, as in sexual abuse and slavery. It is through considering these polluting ties that we understand the idea of sin. There is no such thing as sin in the liberal-individualist picture; people make mistakes, they act wrongly towards each other; but they do not *fall*. They are not *cast out*, as are the fallen angels in *Paradise Lost*. In *Parsifal*, however, we are given a fascinating account of sin, and of its central place in the religious experience. Sin, in *Parsifal*, is an existential pollution, a fall from true and honest being, so as to become the wrong kind of thing.

As the opera shows at every stage, human beings fall into wrong relations with others, leading to guilt and shame. The Grail was given in order to cleanse us of those faults, and to renew our participation in a consecrated life. But the sanctuary of the Grail has been polluted, and one of the sacred relics has been captured and profaned. The pollution of the sanctuary is not felt only by Amfortas, though his pain and remorse are the direct results of it. A profound disquiet has entered the kingdom of the Grail, and this is manifest in the brutal treatment of Kundry by the squires, in the domineering attitude of Titurel and most of all in the almost sadistic abuse of Amfortas in his guilt and agony. We witness a community devoted to the Redeemer which has forgotten the Redeemer's message. Parsifal must retrace the path taken by Amfortas, in order to rescue what was lost. He must undergo the temptation of polluted love, so as to reach through to the love born of compassion, the love taught by the Redeemer. And he must do this not for his own sake, but for the sake of Amfortas and the kingdom of the Grail.

The wrestling with sin, and longing for right relations with others, is one half of the religious experience. But it is not the whole of it. There is also the search for consolation. It is not only death and physical suffering that trouble us in this life; there is the heart's sorrow, the yearning for a love and blessedness that we might have known in childhood, the grief at our fleetingness and the fleetingness of all that we cherish. This sorrow is a true reflection of what we are, and those who do not to some measure feel it are not fully human. All real love brings sorrow to those who are joined by it, and this sorrow attaches to sexual love, to the love of parents and children, to the love of beauty, of country and of the paths and pageants of our youth. Parsifal's mother, whose name, Herzeleide, epitomizes this sorrow, also dies from it, and its nature is incomparably evoked in the Prelude, in the sequence of 'commiserating sevenths'[14] with which it ends. This passage caused Nietzsche (in a letter to Peter Gast of January 1887) to praise the Prelude for its 'sympathy with what is seen and shown forth that cuts through the soul as with a knife ... Has any painter ever depicted so sorrowful a look of love as Wagner does in the final accents of his Prelude?' This sorrowful look of love sounds through the entire score of *Parsifal*, uniting everything that happens. But it raises another and vital question about the Monsalvat religion. In what way and to what extent does this faith, which offers no compensating afterlife, nevertheless console us for our sorrow? And what part is played in this by the sacrifice of a Redeemer who has long ago gone from the world? Answering such questions in words leads always to puzzlement and paradox. But they are answered by the music, which connects suffering and compassion, sin and forgiveness, downfall and redemption, in a web of necessity, healing the fractures and uniting the warring parts of human life in a way that is clear, convincing and uncanny.

The interdependence of sin, sorrow, love and compassion is symbolized at every point in the drama. But symbols are effective only if they have a dramatic life of their own, independently of their symbolic meaning. The characters have to be real before they can be true symbols of anything, themselves included. *Parsifal* owes its power to emotions that are, for all their extremism, inherently believable, and contained in characters that are both vivid and plausible once we make allowance for their miracle-ridden context. Even Parsifal, whose initial condition as a bewildered simpleton poses a special challenge to the dramatist, becomes steadily more lifelike as his education proceeds, and as simplicity and ignorance become knowledge and faith. At the same time the characters, as always in Wagner, exist at the extreme limit of desire and suffering, as though discovering each other in the aftermath of some vast calamity. They are longing, like Kundry, for something that lies beyond the reach of ordinary thought and action, something that will make their vast suffering worthwhile. This deep longing is again given clarity and form by the music, which is an icon of the consecrated life, reaching to the very limit of our prayers in its call for wholeness and healing. It sounds with the voice of Psalm 51: 'The sacrifices of God are a broken spirit; a broken and a contrite heart, O God, Thou wilt not despise.' It yearns beyond that deepest cry of the wounded soul, and also leads, by the highest artistic contrivance, to the musical equivalent of forgiveness and closure. All this, contained in the haunting melody with which the work begins, lifts us out of ordinary time, and tells us that what we really are, in the sacred place of our belonging, leaves a trace in eternity. We are condemned to *chronos* time; but our reality is *kairos*.

2

Wagner's Treatment of the Story

Wagner lifts all of the following from Wolfram's narrative: the king whose wound, inflicted during a sexual transgression, will not heal but is relieved only by bathing and balsam; the chaste fool who knows little or nothing of his origins, not even his name; the mother whom the fool abandons to her grief; the birth of compassion in the fool, through studying the birds that he has shot; the castle of the Grail, which cannot be found by enquiry, but only if the seeker is called there by the Grail itself; the quest for God, answered only in a Good Friday sermon; the order of Grail knights, whose king alone escapes the vow of celibacy, though he then abuses the privilege; the lingering former King Titurel, watching from his tomb-like place of confinement and kept alive by his regular sighting of the Grail; the sacred Spear that brings relief when placed in the wound; Cundrie, the messenger of the Grail, riding along mysterious pathways, appearing now at the castle of the Grail, now in distant regions, now in the Schastel Marveil of the magician Clinschor, and who seems to have knowledge of Parzival's mother and of other aspects of his life; the castrated magician with his enchanted precinct, where knights and ladies are confined for his entertainment. Most importantly Wagner follows Wolfram in creating a hero who wanders in a state of bewilderment and guilt – guilt over matters about which he learns only in retrospect, and only when it is too late for any immediate remedy.

In all these, Wagner manages somehow both to respect Wolfram's narrative and also to provide it with a deeper meaning. Two additions to the story aid him in this: first the demonic character of Kundry, who becomes central to the action, and the person on whom everything ultimately turns; secondly the explicitly Eucharistic interpretation of the Grail. Although *Parzifal* is a Christian poem, the distinction between Christian and heathen is neither dwelt upon nor properly spelled out in Wolfram's narrative. No mass is celebrated, priesthood gets only a passing mention, and the hermit Trevrizent belongs to no specific order. The Grail is not connected with the Passion of Christ, and its benefits seem to be largely material – good food and wine, an extra week of earthly life, luxury accommodation.

Baptism occurs towards the end of the story, when Parzifal's half-brother Firefiz cheerfully submits to it in order to gain the hand of the conductress of the Grail, Queen Repanse de Schoye. But the rituals that occur are mostly arcane mysteries, one involving a mysterious bleeding spear, which point beyond the clearly marked-out territory of religious observance. Heathen beliefs are barely discussed, and are in any case of no great importance, involving deities from the Roman canon who are clearly on the way out: certainly there is no recognition of Islam as a rival to Christianity and an alternative answer to the *zwîvel* that torments the hero.[1] And the manifestly un-Christian nature of the jousts and pledges, in which death is administered without remorse, so long as etiquette is followed, and honour and manly display trump every other purpose, seems hardly to bother any of the characters save Herzeloyde, and even she is nonplussed when it comes to explaining the matter to her son.

Wagner's response is to place a version of the Christian religion in the centre of the drama, not as a doctrine, but as a sacrament that establishes the frame within which everything occurs. Parzifal's original puzzlement – 'What is God?' – is brought to earth in other forms ('Who is good?', 'Who is the Grail?'), and in the speechless compassion that prompts the search for knowledge. As in Wolfram the quest does not precede the discovery: the discovery precedes the quest, which is not for the Grail, but for the Spear, Companion to the Grail, whose loss has brought about the destruction of the Grail kingdom, and whose return will spell the restoration of the community and the healing of its king.

The Grail literature may well have roots, as Wagner thought, in oriental sources, and in Wolfram's version the Grail bears the mark of a meteorite cult, such as existed in Muhammad's day around the holy stone of the Ka'ba, thrown from Heaven as a sign to mankind. The reverence for this stone is the one fragment of his pagan upbringing that the Prophet adhered to, and forms the centre of the pilgrimage to which all his followers are adjured. *Graal*, however, does not mean stone. It is Old French for a bowl, or similar vessel (Latin *gradalis*, Greek *krater*). For Chrétien de Troyes, in *Perceval: li Conte del Graal*, written around 1190 and the inspiration for Wolfram's epic, the Grail is a tray or salver, and in Robert de Boron's *Joseph d'Arimathie*, written around the same time, it is identified with the vessel used by Christ at the Last Supper, and also by Joseph of Arimathea to collect the blood of Christ at the Crucifixion. The theme of the Holy Chalice is continued in the so-called 'Vulgate Cycle', the 'Post-Vulgate Cycle' and Thomas Malory's *Le Morte d'Arthur*. And in due course the chalice acquired a companion – the lance that pierced the side of Christ at the Crucifixion, and which is said in the apocryphal Gospel of Nicodemus to have been wielded by the centurion Longinus. This 'lance of Longinus' has had a chequered history as a holy relic, with many candidates still preserved and revered across the Christian world.[2]

The medieval cult of relics is a subject of frequent mockery, not least because of its commercial abuse by the Church. However, the idea of a relic goes to the heart of the religion invoked in *Parsifal*. The Grail castle is a place once visited by angels and containing the gift brought down by them from Heaven. The Redeemer has left his trace in the world, and by seeking it we become closer to him, and also closer to seeing the world in another light, as the place of our salvation. Christian pilgrims follow in the footsteps of Christ, and to discover the props that feature in his holy story is to see what he saw, and to touch what he touched, so becoming more vividly convinced that he moves among us still. A relic is a kind of divine guarantee of the somewhere where we are, and the possession of a relic has always been a sign of the legitimacy and permanence of a human settlement, even if the relic has to be captured and brought from elsewhere, like the body of St Mark brought to Venice from Alexandria.

At the same time, a relic from the Gospel story, because it has been *left* in this world, is also a sign of Christ's other-worldly character: it is not just left, but left behind. It points away from this world, to the no-place outside time, whither the Redeemer has retreated. Hence relics, which authenticate a place as *somewhere*, also have the aura of *nowhere*; being close to them you are to that extent removed from this world. A kind of contagious magic attaches to them, and communities who guard some relic, shielding it from profanation, also see themselves as tied in a bond of obedience, a *religio* in what some take to be the original meaning of the term. They are *servants* of the relic, as the knights of Monsalvat are servants of the Grail.

All this is delicately rehearsed in Wagner's narrative. We are brought to understand the otherworldly character of Monsalvat, which can appear anywhere and at any time. At this very moment you might stumble into it, fail to ask the question for which it is waiting, and so return to ordinary things unaware that you have just missed the chance of salvation. The *kairos* moment sinks away, ordinary time and space close over it and, looking back across the unruffled surface of your life, you find no trace of 'what might have been', the moment when you yourself were called.

Parsifal has the form of a triptych. Acts I and III are set in Monsalvat, Act II in the magic castle of Klingsor. The main characters stand outlined and face to face as in a painting. If there is movement it is the place that moves and not the people, unless the people are simply features of the place, like the knights and flower-maidens. The action represented on the stage occurs at no *chronos* time; like the Eucharist it is a 'point of intersection of the timeless with time', always recurring, never past.

The melody in A flat major that opens the Prelude (1, the *Grund-thema*) weaves together threads associated with communion, longing, pain and salvation in a seamless evocation of the religious way of life.[3] It is repeated beneath a shimmering accompaniment, and then followed by a silence, the first of many. In the religious way of life, we understand, silence is always resumed. We are then given the *Grund-thema* in C minor (1A), followed by plain statements of the Grail and faith motifs (2, 3), framed by the same silence, before the *Grundthema* is taken apart and dissolved in sorrow. Even before the curtain rises we feel that we are entering a grieving and imploring world. The

Prelude ends with a dominant seventh chord, accumulating over eight bars, like the heartfelt prayer of a community, calling for the one who will rescue it. But the chord is left unresolved, the orchestra again falls silent and, as the curtain rises, we hear only trombones on stage, repeating the first notes of the opening phrase of the Prelude at a major third below.

This is the call to morning prayer, and the good-natured knight Gurnemanz now adds his voice to it, teasing two young squires awake in preparation for their daily duty. Nothing could possibly more lighten the burden of such a Prelude than Gurnemanz's plainspoken wake-up call, invoking God's presence and – with the bluff stoicism of an old soldier – bracing his hearers for the appearance of their wounded king.

After praying with them in silence, Gurnemanz commands the two squires to see to the bath of the king, whose cortège is now approaching. We hear the motif of Amfortas (8), which wobbles on its augmented triad as though every note were a jolt of pain. Two knights enter and Gurnemanz asks them how the king fares, and whether the balsam skilfully won by Gawan has brought some relief. He is reproached for his optimism, and told of the king's sleepless night and of the pain that has returned more fiercely than ever. Subdued, Gurnemanz says: we are fools to seek a cure through balsam, when only one person can help.

The orchestra gives out the first two bars of the motif of prophecy (9A), which seems to emerge softly from the reference to fools. Only later does the motif appear in its completed form, setting the words:

> Durch Mitleid wissend
> der reine Tor,
> harre sein
> den ich erkor.

'Knowing through compassion, the pure fool: await him, the one I chose.' The four crucial words in this description of the Grail kingdom's saviour – *Mitleid*, *wissend*, *reine*, *Tor* – are each steeped in philosophy, and my aim is to explain that philosophy as best I can. Bewildered, the knights ask for the name of this pure fool, but Gurnemanz evades the question.

The conversation is interrupted by the young squires, pointing excitedly off stage. We hear the motif of riding (10A), as they describe the wild Kundry, galloping towards them and now falling to the ground from her exhausted mare. She rushes in, dressed in wild garb, her black hair loose and dishevelled, her skirts gathered by a snake-skin girdle. The stage directions tell us that her eyes are dark and piercing, sometimes flashing wildly, more often strangely fixed and staring. The music to which she enters – a fortissimo dissonance, leading to a cascade on strings over three and a half octaves (11) – is associated at first with Kundry's wild nature and with her sudden demonic laughter, though gradually it acquires a wider significance, becoming the voice of disorder in a world that is falling apart.

She runs to Gurnemanz and presses a small crystal phial into his hand saying brusquely 'Here, take this! Balsam . . .' (12). In reply to Gurnemanz's question she says that she found it further off than his mind can reach: if this does not work, she adds, then Arabia offers nothing else that will. 'Ask no further,' she says and throws herself to the ground, declaring that she is weary.

Here, in the space of a few bars, and with bold musical strokes, Wagner gives us the wild character of Kundry, her miraculous way of transporting herself, her connection with Arabia and its magical potions, the soothing balm for which she rejects all thanks and her schizophrenic cries that sound like laughter, but which are the screams of inner demons. Her mostly silent presence on the stage puts an indelible mark on all that follows.

The cortège of knights and squires now enters, bearing the litter of the stricken king. As they approach, Gurnemanz gives way to lamen-tations, recalling the proud manhood of the king (13) and his enslavement by the sickness that now causes him to groan in pain. Gurnemanz urges the squires to be more gentle with the litter, as Amfortas raises himself slightly in order to gain sight of the holy lake. The wild night of pain, he says, now yields to the light of morning, and the orchestra relinquishes themes of suffering for a breezy melody (14) that seems to float across the scene from the surface of the lake: though not for long, since the memory of the night of pain returns with a phrase that foreshadows much – both musical and emotional – that still awaits us:

The groan of pain, captured in the falling phrase here, above the
three-note accented up-beat of the Spear motif (5), points forward to
the subsequent harrowing depictions of the king's distress. Already,
we learn, Amfortas's authority is weakening, since Gawan has
departed in search of another balm without permission (and in danger, Amfortas reminds the knights, from Klingsor's snares). But the
king does not dwell on the matter; instead, in his desperation, he
allows his thoughts to wander to the promise of rescue, once issued
from the Grail. We hear again the first part of the prophecy motif
(9A), interrupted now by Gurnemanz, as he steps forward to offer the
phial of balsam brought from Arabia. (Here, as before, the reference
to Arabia is accompanied by a chromatic phrase, 12A, from the *Tristan* lexicon, associated there with Brangäne's casket of magic potions.)

Amfortas asks who brought the balsam, and Gurnemanz replies
'There lies the wild maid. Up, Kundry, come!' 'You, Kundry?' asks
Amfortas, 'Do I have to thank you again?', to which her response is
another demonic shriek as she writhes on the ground, refusing to be
thanked. Amfortas gives the signal to his entourage to proceed, and
they make their way down to the water, first to the painful theme of
Amfortas's procession, and then to the airy melody (14) already associated with the lake.

Gurnemanz gazes after the cortège sadly while Kundry, still lying
on the ground, is abused by two of the squires as a savage beast. 'Are
not the beasts here holy?' she responds, but the squires are suspicious of her magic powers and continue to berate her. Gurnemanz
intercedes on her behalf. He points out that she carries messages to

the knights fighting in distant lands, demands neither food nor lodging, and is always ready to help in emergencies. But she is a heathen, a sorceress, they reply, and Gurnemanz suggests that perhaps she lives under a curse, maybe guilt for some fault committed in an earlier life, which she seeks to expiate through her service to the brotherhood of knights. As this thought takes shape in Gurnemanz's faltering words the orchestra gives out the *Grundthema* in the minor (1A), leading not to the pain-filled second phrase but rather to the prophecy motif (9A).

Gradually, as the story of Monsalvat unfolds, and the prophecy motif emerges into the foreground, we understand that it is not saying one thing only: it is the voice of the Grail itself – the voice that haunts this sacred precinct, speaking of things too deep for common observation, things 'hidden since the foundation of the world' (Matthew 13:35).[4] It is from among those things that the pure fool will finally come with the gift of salvation. The truth about Kundry is also one of those hidden things. It is not known to ordinary observation, but can be discerned only by the kind of intuition that escapes from the present moment, so as to reach into *kairos* time.

In the outline of the drama contained in his diary for 29 August 1865 Wagner described Kundry's transition from Klingsor's castle, the no-place of her sinful triumph, to Monsalvat, the no-place of her contrition: 'From one state to the next she carries no real consciousness of what has passed: to her it is like a dream experienced in very deep sleep which, on waking, one has no recollection of, only a vague, impotent feeling prevailing deep down inside. Yet she gazes with both sadness and scorn at the wounded man [Amfortas], whom she, penitent now, again serves with most passionate devotion, but – without hope, without respect.'[5] Certainly Amfortas does not know that the Kundry of Monsalvat is the seductress of Klingsor's castle, although he has had direct acquaintance with them both.

Gurnemanz, thinking aloud, remembers that Amfortas's wound occurred when Kundry was away from Monsalvat. He recalls Titurel's original discovery of the wild woman, numb and lifeless in the undergrowth, as he set out to build the castle that would be the shrine of the Grail (7A). Gurnemanz too had discovered her in that lifeless state, after the disaster of the Spear, the music now backing him up with the mesmerizing theme of Kundry's enchantment (15). Kundry and the Grail are mysteriously connected, and her presence just there, in the no-place to which the Grail has been brought from nowhere, exhibits the spiritual necessity that binds all that happens in Monsalvat. Of this too Gurnemanz has an inkling. He turns to her now with a blunt question: 'Hey you! Where were you wandering when our lord lost the Spear? Why didn't you help on *that* day?' To which she replies 'I never help.' 'There you are,' the squires conclude: 'ask her to go and get the Spear.'

'That is for another,' replies Gurnemanz gloomily: 'the task is denied to us.' The second fragment of the *Grundthema*, the theme of pain (4), has steadily crept into the foreground, together with the motif of the Spear (5). Gurnemanz recalls the Spear with deepest feeling, remembering the unholy hand in which it was held when last he saw it. He tells the story of Amfortas's enchantment, in the attempt on Klingsor's castle, by a fearfully beautiful woman, who caused him to let go of the Spear. The music of enchantment moves to a crisis that spills over into pain and revulsion, in a sequence (16) that will later accompany Parsifal as he savours and then starts away from Kundry's kiss. A deathly cry, Gurnemanz recalls, brought him running to assist his lord, but the laughing Klingsor had disappeared with the Spear, leaving the wound that will never heal. As Gurnemanz recounts this we hear the concluding phrase of the *Grundthema*, as this had been woefully elaborated at the end of the Prelude (5 and 6).

Squires return from the lake with the news that the king has been a little eased by Kundry's balsam. Gurnemanz responds to the request that he recount what he knows of Klingsor. He tells how Titurel, who had defended the realm of faith against evil forces, was visited one solemn night by the Saviour's angels, bringing the Cup of the Last Supper, used at the Crucifixion to collect his sacred blood, together with the Spear by which the blood was shed. The theme of the angels (17), melded with the Grail motif (2), introduces the *Grundthema*, as Gurnemanz expounds the mystery of the Grail. The Grail summons to its precinct those with purity of heart, in order that they may work the will of Heaven. Here, for the first time, the Grail motif is given a full symphonic elaboration, in music that expresses the solidarity and mutual comfort of the brotherhood of knights.

This beautiful passage of diatonic polyphony gives way abruptly to the chromatic motif, 18, associated with Klingsor, as Gurnemanz tells the story of the Grail's enemy. Klingsor longed to join the order of the Grail, perhaps in atonement for some sin committed in those heathen lands beyond the nearby valley where he has raised his home. Unable to surmount the lust that constantly tormented him, Klingsor turned on himself a sinful mutilating hand, so causing Titurel to reject him from the sacred order. Afire with rage, Klingsor discovered how his shameful deed opened a path to evil powers, which he used to raise a magic garden in the desert, where devilish lovely women (19) tempt the Grail knights to evil and polluting joys, so that the knights remain there, with Klingsor as master. When Titurel, stricken with age, passed the lordship of the Grail to his son, Amfortas, the latter departed at once, in order to bring an end to this plague, taking with him the holy Spear. However, because of Amfortas's seduction by the beautiful woman whom he encountered in Klingsor's domain, the wizard now possesses the Spear, using it to wound the Grail knights and hoping soon to win the Grail. Meanwhile Amfortas lay before the violated sanctuary in fervent prayer, entreating for a sign of forgiveness. A sacred radiance lit up the Grail and a holy dream-image appeared, with words of mystic meaning shining before Amfortas: 'Knowing through compassion, the pure fool, wait for him, the one I chose' (9A and B).

The four squires who have been listening to this story repeat the first part of the prophecy, whose arresting intervals and chord sequence have now been woven into the work's harmonic fabric. Cries of alarm from the lake cut the prophecy short, and squires and knights enter in agitation as a wild swan flutters to the ground, pierced by an arrow. Who shot the swan? asks Gurnemanz. A knight recounts that the king greeted the sight of the swan, circling above the lake, as a happy omen. Parsifal is led in, gripping his bow and arrow, and the knights surround and accuse him. Was it you? asks Gurnemanz, to which the orchestra replies with Parsifal's motif, 21, the boy affirming that he shoots everything that flies. Gurnemanz responds with a sermon, dwelling on the harmless woodland creatures that are Parsifal's friends, on the birds above him in the branches, and on the swan, circling the lake in search of his mate – and here the orchestra quotes the swan motif from *Lohengrin* (20).

As the old knight points to the wound, the blood, the drooping wings and glazed eye of the swan, the orchestra makes the connection with Amfortas's pain. With growing emotion Parsifal breaks his bow, throws the arrows away and passes a hand over his eyes, Gurnemanz still urging his guilt. Then, in response to questions, the boy reveals that he knows neither the identity of his father, nor how he came to Monsalvat, nor even his name – of which he had many, all forgotten. We hear at this point, for the first time, the exquisitely tender motif of Herzeleide, 22, harmonized in four parts on divided cellos. This is Wagner's way of evoking a touching moment in Wolfram's story, when Parzifal, asked for his name, remembers only being called 'bon fîz, scher fîz, beâ fîz' (good son, dear son, beautiful son).

The swan, lifted reverently on to a bier of fresh branches, is carried away by some of the squires, while others repair to assist the king at the lakeside. Gurnemanz and Parsifal remain on stage, with Kundry lying apart. You must remember *something*, Gurnemanz says, and in response the boy recalls his mother, his childhood in the forest, the bow and arrow that he made for himself. Gurnemanz wonders why Parsifal's mother did not provide him with more appropriate weapons, for clearly the boy was born of noble stock. At this Kundry raucously interrupts with the account of Parsifal's father's death and Herzeleide's policy of raising the boy apart from the world, so making a fool of him, a point underlined by the opening chords of the prophecy motif, 9A.

Parsifal enthusiastically joins in with Kundry's story, referring to his encounter with a troop of knights in the forest, his pursuit of them, wanting to be like them, and becoming lost in wild places, forced to defend himself with his bow and arrow from both beasts and men. This passage, beginning with a childlike 'Yes!' from Parsifal as he spills out his story, involves a subtle synthesis of Kundry's riding motif (10) and Parsifal's signature theme (21). The music conveys both the vulnerable innocence of Parsifal, and the secret knowledge possessed by the woman who has been tracking his life. There is an eerie suggestion that it is Kundry who has led the boy to the Grail. She, the messenger of the Grail in the old story, also has a part in the Grail's sacred purpose. Once again we glimpse the ties of necessity that bind the people, the objects and the events that unfold in Monsalvat.

Kundry rises to her feet during this narrative. The boy soon taught robbers and giants to fear him, Kundry says, and this leads Parsifal to ask 'Who fears me?' 'Die Bösen,' she replies: the wicked. Reflecting on this Parsifal asks another question: 'Who is good?' The melodic sequence here, 23, is, according to Alfred Lorenz, a core motif, returning in many contexts, and bearing a weight of significance; it is the voice of 'the ethical question'. (I return to this suggestion in Chapter 5 below.)

To the question of who is good Gurnemanz answers: 'Your mother, whom you deserted, and who now grieves for you.' Kundry corrects him: 'Her grief is ended: his mother is dead', at which Parsifal starts up in alarm and disbelief, gripping Kundry by the throat as though he would strangle her. Gurnemanz restrains him, saying that Kundry sees much and never lies, at which Parsifal is seized with a violent trembling and declares that he is about to faint. Kundry hastens to a nearby spring and returns with a horn, from which she sprinkles water on Parsifal before giving it to him to drink. Gurnemanz comments that this is the way of the Grail, to return evil with good. The orchestra adds the motif of service/balsam (12) but Kundry rejects the condescending verdict, saying 'I never do good', as the theme of her enchantment, 15, stirs in the orchestra. She is weary, she feels the call to sleep, but no! she cries, not sleep. And the Klingsor motif, 18, edges closer. She collapses behind a bush, muttering 'Sleep, sleep I must'.

Up to this point the stage has been occupied by as much telling as showing, with succinct characterizations set against a background of narrative. Henceforth things move in another way. Gurnemanz puts his arm around Parsifal and leads him to the feast of the Grail, the music maintaining a steady march to 24A and B, as the scenery moves behind the stepping figures. Gurnemanz has told Parsifal, in answer to the latter's question, that the holy vessel can be found only by the one whom the Grail itself has chosen, adding that here time becomes space; in other words, that in Monsalvat you enter *kairos* time. Gurnemanz suspects that the person beside him as they travel is the one foretold in the prophecy, and the wonderful transformation music encapsulates the yearning and suffering of the desecrated

shrine as it beckons to the pure fool who is to rescue it. Heard thrice
in this purely orchestral episode is the theme of woe (25) that Robin
Holloway[6] describes as the work's central sonorous image:

It is clear that the approach to the Grail is through the darkest heart of
grief and suffering. As the walls of rock open to reveal the mighty hall
of the Grail temple, Gurnemanz turns to the astonished Parsifal and
declares 'Pay good heed; if you are a fool and pure, let me see what
knowledge may come to you here.' The knights of the Grail then enter
from the right and range themselves at the tables of the feast. They refer
to 'the latest love-feast, renewed from day to day', and invite others to
draw near and partake of the food 'as at the last time' (27). (Playing on
the words 'zum letzten Male' Wagner suggests that this is the present
offering of a meal that is always renewed and always the last: an idea
enshrined in the Christian conception of the Last Supper.) The knights
add that the meal is reserved for those who rejoice in good deeds.

So far Wagner's Grail-feast resembles Wolfram's: a convivial
dinner in the college hall. But, as the covered shrine of the Grail is
brought in by four squires, leading Amfortas on his litter, the music
takes on a darker character, with the motifs of suffering and contrition (5A, 5B and 6) coming to the fore. The young novices, halfway
up the dome of the temple, respond to the manly invitation of the
knights with a chromatic reflection on the Redeemer's blood, in
which we are given a first glimpse of the *Parsifal* theology:

> Den sündigen Welten
> mit tausend Schmerzen.
> wie einst sein Blut geflossen,

> dem Erlösungshelden
> sei nun mit freudigem Herzen
> mein Blut vergossen:
> der Leib, den Er zur Sühn' uns bot,
> er leb' in uns durch seinen Tod!

(For the sins of the world, with a thousand sorrows, as once His blood flowed, so may I now offer my blood to the redeeming hero with joyful heart: the body that He as atonement gave us lives in us through His death.)

The music here is put together from the various cries of woe (25), though in a more plangent and pitying form, as though to remind us that our suffering is of no account beside the sorrow of the Redeemer. The lament is rounded off with the Grail motif, after which the pages add their comment from the summit of the dome, now in the simple, mesmerizing melody of the faith motif:

> Der Glaube lebt,
> die Taube schwebt,
> des Heilands holder Bote:
> der für euch fliesst,
> des Weines geniesst,
> und nehmt vom Lebens-Brote!

(Faith lives, the dove hovers, the Saviour's lovely messenger: drink the wine that flows for you, and take from the Bread of Life!)

While Wagner's words acknowledge that the Redeemer has died in atonement for our sins, and point to His mystical presence in the bread and wine of communion, they make no claims about the Resurrection, affirming only that 'He lives in us through His death.' The question is: how? Thus begins Parsifal's quest, and ours.

When all have taken their place there is a moment of silence, the most pregnant silence in all opera. It is broken by the unaccompanied voice of Titurel, coming from a vaulted niche behind the couch of Amfortas, as though from a tomb. 'My son, Amfortas,' he calls, 'are you ready?' Silence. 'Shall I see the Grail today and live?' Silence. 'Must I then die, unguided by the Saviour?' These heartless questions are answered at last, by Amfortas's cries of woe, in the poignant orchestration that had burst through the tissue of the transformation music like a wild beast through a paper wall. Amfortas begs Titurel, just this once, to resume the office that he has passed to his son, but Titurel replies that he is too weak to serve, and that Amfortas must atone for his sin. 'Reveal the Grail!' he commands; the squires start forward for the ceremony, but Amfortas restrains them, crying 'No! Leave it unrevealed!'

The motifs of contrition and woe wrestle together, as Amfortas prays 'may no one know the burning pain that I suffer at the holy sight for which you long – I the only sinner entreating the blessing of the Grail on my sinless brothers! For Him, for His holy greeting, my heart yearns, in deepest repentance. The time is near, a beam of light falls on the shrine, the covering falls.' The Grail theme, which has superseded the depiction of Amfortas's pain, now gives way to the *Grundthema* under tremolo strings, as Amfortas describes the blood shining in the holy vessel, flowing too in his heart, but his own pol-luted blood recoils in shame from it, gushing out into the world of sin and lust. Amfortas's wound has opened, 'a wound like His, inflicted by the Spear that wounded Him'. He cries out with pain and remorse, lamenting this flow of sinful blood, renewed by the tide of yearning that no repentance stills. In his moral and physical agony he appeals for mercy, begging for a death that will put him again in right rel-ation to the all-merciful one whom he addresses.

The music, having explored the extremes of mental and physical pain, collapses into the sorrowful cadence from the end of the Prelude, as Amfortas begs with faltering words, before sinking back as if unconscious. The pages and squires pronounce the prophecy, unaccom-panied, from halfway up the dome, and the knights join in, reminding Amfortas of what has been promised, and urging him to fulfil his office now. Titurel repeats the order to reveal the Grail, Amfortas raises himself with difficulty, and the acolytes uncover the golden shrine, taking from it the crystal chalice of the Grail. They remove its cover and place it before Amfortas. The communion ceremony begins.

This repeats the opening music of the Prelude, the *Grundthema* now slightly adapted to accommodate the syllables of the communion words, as reworked by Wagner. These are sung first by the novice knights, then by the pages from on high:

Nehmet hin meinen Leib
nehmet hin mein Blut
um unsrer Liebe willen.

Nehmet hin mein Blut
nehmet hin meinen Leib,
auf dass ihr mein' gedenkt.

('Take my body, take my blood, for the sake of our love; Take my
blood, take my body, in remembrance of me': words directly derived
from those recorded by St Paul in 1 Corinthians 11:23–6, and used in
all Christian communion services.) The C minor version of the
Grundthema moves beautifully behind its shimmering accompaniment, lapsing into the themes of sorrow and the Spear (6, 5) as
Amfortas raises the Grail and waves it gently to every side. Titurel
declares his rapture at the sight of it: 'How brightly does the Lord
greet us today!' – the very same Lord, we note, the 'all merciful' one,
who has just failed to grant mercy to Titurel's son.

Amfortas blesses two flagons of wine and baskets of bread by waving the Grail above them, and four squires now distribute the bread
and fill the cups of the assembled company, while the communion
hymn is sung (28). This hymn gives us another fragment of the *Parsifal* theology. It tells us that the bread and wine of the Last Supper
were changed into the flesh and blood of the Redeemer's sacrifice,
and are now changed back to bread and wine in the feast of love. The
knights then invite those receiving the bread to turn it again to
flesh, brave unto death and steadfast in working the will of the
Saviour, while inviting them to change the wine into the fiery blood
of life, joining the knights as brothers in the holy fight. Just how far
all this is from the orthodox Christian communion is a matter to
which I return; but the marching melody, 28, already implies much
about the relation between the knights and their king, who has so
horribly suffered in order to renew their boisterous fellowship. With
the words 'blessed in faith and love', sung by all, the communion
ends, Amfortas now sunk down on his couch and pressing his wound
in pain. He is attended to by the squires before being carried away,
followed by the assembled company, marching to the theme already
heard in the transformation music, the cries of woe (25) three times

bursting through the orchestral texture. The temple empties and only Gurnemanz and Parsifal remain, the boy standing shocked and motionless, his hand pressed to his heart.

'What are you doing standing there?' asks Gurnemanz, 'Do you know what you just saw?' The cries of woe sound again from the orchestra as Parsifal clutches his heart. 'You are indeed a fool,' says Gurnemanz in irritation. Opening a side door he pushes the boy from the temple, telling him to leave the swans alone since he is only a goose. From the height of the dome an alto voice sings the first part of the Prophecy, and the scene ends as altos and sopranos sing 'Selig im Glauben', 'Blessed in faith'.

A convention arose, beginning with the first productions of the work in Bayreuth, that the audience should not applaud but remain silent at the end of this first Act. The convention was a response to an overwhelming experience, whose power does not derive only from artistic contrivance and supremely beautiful music, or from the visceral associations of the Christian Eucharist, here presented in full pontifical splendour, but – more importantly – from the incorporation into the Eucharist of a real sacrificial victim. There at the centre of the drama is a human being in agony, prostrate before the altar from which the congregation is fed, as though fed from his blood. God the father is not mentioned, all thoughts turn to death and suffering, and everything said and done is as though soaked in blood. Wagner has returned the Eucharist to its dark original, the ceremony with which a community must, with unceasing regularity, claim divine protection, seek atonement for its sins, and, in the urgency of its need, sacrifice a victim so that the blood of life should flow.

Lévi-Strauss praised Wagner as the founder of structural anthropology.[7] But the composer anticipated the mimetic theory of René Girard too, not to speak of the insights of Mary Douglas in her studies of pollution and taboo.[8] He understood, as few before or after him have understood, that the sacred, the sacrificial and the sacramental are aspects of a single world-changing endeavour: the endeavour for which 'redemption' was Wagner's name. He had the uncanny ability to explore beneath our sophisticated rituals, in order to discover their roots in the pre-history of humankind. And in doing so he revealed what our rituals mean.

Wagner regarded the concept of the sacred as indispensable to human relations. But he also believed that it is we who render things sacred, and that no God has a part in it. A central theme of *Parsifal*, therefore, is the way in which we sanctify ('make sacred') what most concerns us, and how this making sacred is a collective achievement, which cannot easily be rectified when something goes wrong. To explain all this in words would undermine the drama. But it can be presented clearly in music, and that is what Wagner does. By using the sublime melody of the *Grundthema* for the communion words, and repeating the melody beneath its shimmering accompaniment, Wagner presents an unforgettable distillation of the religious moment. The music conveys the complete surrender of the participant's being to the ritual, while carrying a burden of suffering implanted in the notes. It shows us why the knights, observing their ruined king, cannot simply conclude that it would be better to put a stop to Holy Communion, to dissolve the Order, and to bury the Grail in some place where it can do no harm. A community that has been 'made sacred' has undergone an existential change, from which there is no turning back. There is no alternative for the Grail knights but to rescue the missing relic from the profane hands that pollute it, while renewing the sanctity of their Order as best they can.

Wagner's music always rises to the great moments of human aspiration, as in this communion ceremony. But he was a meticulous observer of small things too, and recognized the way in which the great and the small depend on each other. In every Catholic church, after the sacrament of the mass, when the priest has pronounced the words 'Ite, missa est' or some vernacular equivalent such as 'Go in peace', and the communicants have begun to take their leave, there is a moment of ordinary housekeeping, a shuffling of figures behind the altar, a tidying of sacred vessels and an opening and closing of sacristy doors. Far from negating the otherworldly character of the mass this quiet bustle domesticates the ritual, showing us that the sacred moment occurs in ordinary life and is continuous with it. This familiar experience is beautifully captured at the end of Act I of *Parsifal*, in the moment of Gurnemanz's everyday impatience, before the voices high above give out a last echo of the sacred event.

The medieval Church established communities of renunciation, some, like the monastic orders, devoted to charity and prayer, some, like the Knights Templar, to the defence of Christendom against the infidel. Irreligion, for those communities, was not atheism, but a rival and debased form of religion, known as sorcery or magic, and associated with the heathen culture of Arabia. Religion tells us that we do not have power over the world, and that we must learn to accept our limitations and to recognize that our salvation depends on the God who will rescue us. When we pray we do not command the world to obey us; on the contrary, we humbly acknowledge our lack of power, and ask God to intervene on our behalf. Prayer is a recognition of our weakness, and a resolve at the same time to deserve God's help.

In this respect prayers are the very opposite of spells. The one who casts a spell is assuming power over reality. He has no need of God since he *is* God: he is assuming the powers of the creator and subduing life and matter to his will. Magic, in this sense, is a kind of blasphemy, and when alchemy was condemned by the medieval Church it was as an attempt to dispense with God.[9]

Similar thoughts inspire the dramatic use of magic both by Goethe in *Faust* and by Wagner in the second Act of *Parsifal*. The sorcerer, according to the medieval view of things, attempts to seize creation from the hand of God and to turn it in another direction, mixing elements that do not belong, diverting nature from its intrinsic end, and remaking the world in the image of the one who abuses it. This mixing of things that do not belong is, according to Mary Douglas, the fundamental character of spiritual pollution, as this is conceived in tribal cultures.[10] And it is of a piece with the existential disorder that Wagner wishes to portray in its most piercing form in *Parsifal*.

This existential disorder is the theme of Act II, which opens with lower strings tumultuously stirring the depths of B minor, while the chromatic motif of Klingsor (18) weaves B minor and G minor together in an obsessive reiteration from which there is no escape. At a certain point one of the cries of woe (25A), Kundry's enchantment and scream (15, 11) and the jagged motif of Klingsor (18) are brought together, in a musical amalgam that shows Amfortas and Kundry as equal victims of the devilish sorcery that has infected them:

The cry of woe is repeated several times, ending with the scream (11) in its full version, as Klingsor casts his habitual spell over Kundry, bending her to the work of spiritual destruction.

The ensuing scene, one of Wagner's psychological master strokes, shows a demonic character revelling in the destruction of joys that he cannot share, who thrives by exploiting another's sexuality in ways that humiliate and enslave her. The audience grasps at once that this is a person who has lost his soul, whose being is so thoroughly polluted as to be a kind of negation of being, an active triumph of nothingness. The spectacle of his remorseless domination of Kundry, and his voyeuristic triumph in her seductions, opens the door to a more forgiving and pitying attitude to the woman whose fatal flaw he exploits. Whatever else we take away from this opening scene it is the sense that spiritual pollution exists in many forms, and that there is more than one way to lose your soul.

The Act opens with Klingsor in his tower of spells, staring into a magic mirror (a detail indirectly lifted from Wolfram). Klingsor perceives the pure fool childishly laughing as he approaches the magic castle. He also perceives Kundry, held in deathly slumber by her curse, and cries 'Quick, to work!', since it is she who is needed for the task in hand, which is to capture Parsifal and destroy him. He summons Kundry with words that invoke her multiple natures. 'To me! Your master calls! First she-devil, Rose of Hell, Herodias you were, and what else? Gundryggia there, Kundry here!'

Gundryggia is the name of a Valkyrie, while the identification with Herodias connects Kundry to Heine's poem of Herodias and the wild hunt, to Flaubert's story of Herodias in his *Trois contes*, and also to the story of John the Baptist. In this respect Kundry exhibits a well-known romantic archetype, revisited by Oscar Wilde and Richard

Strauss in the character of Herodias's daughter, Salomé. According to the medieval legend Herodias, having commanded the decapitation of John the Baptist, lifted the head from the platter in order to implant a kiss on its lips, whereupon a wind, issuing from the Baptist's mouth, blew her around the world for ever. In Wagner's version Kundry is condemned to wander the world in punishment for mocking the Redeemer in his sorrow. This version, borrowing from the legend of Ahasuerus, the 'Wandering Jew', which had already inspired the libretto for *Der fliegende Holländer*, is put forward as evidence for the idea, pursued by Gutman and others, that Kundry represents the Jewish race and its assault on Aryan purity.[11] Such a view of course overlooks Kundry's Nordic credentials as Gundryggia the Valkyrie.

In the blue light that illuminates the stage Kundry's figure appears, seemingly asleep. The orchestra accompanies her appearance with the descending chromatic sequence in parallel thirds, 25A, one of the cries of woe from Monsalvat. She starts up with a blood-curdling shriek. 'Awake?' cries Klingsor, 'Then my spell has worked, at the right time!' To which Kundry responds with a loud wail of misery. Klingsor taunts her, asking where she has been roaming: Still with that rabble of knights though they treat you like a beast? Don't you fare better with me? And when for me you conquered their Master, the holy guardian of the Grail: what drove you to seek them again?

Kundry responds to these taunts with monosyllabic groans, calling on sleep and death. So did someone else awake you? Klingsor asks, to which she replies 'Yes, my curse', and then 'Yearning, yearning' ('Sehnen . . . Sehnen'). 'Yearning for the chaste knights?' asks Klingsor sarcastically. She replies that there she served ('da dient ich'). And Klingsor continues his sarcastic commentary, implying that she seeks to compensate the knights for the great evil she did to them. But that can avail nothing, the strongest will fall, he says, sinking in your embraces to be felled by the Spear that I seized from their king. Today, he adds, you must meet the most dangerous of them all, one shielded by his folly.

Kundry declares, to the motif of sorrow and contrition, 5B, that she *will* not, but he returns that she will because she must. 'By what power do you compel me?' she asks, to which he replies 'I compel you because I am immune to your power.' 'Ha ha,' she responds, taunting him in her turn. 'Are you chaste?' This releases an explosion of bitterness from Klingsor, who recalls the pangs of lust that caused him to mutilate himself, and 'which now rise to mock me aloud through you, you devil's bride!' He threatens her, reminding her that Titurel paid dearly for driving Klingsor from his side, that Titurel's son too has fallen, and that he, Klingsor, will soon possess the Grail. Then he taunts her again, asking 'Was he to your taste, Amfortas the hero, whom I procured for your pleasure?'

This causes Kundry to collapse in sorrow, crying 'Alas, is that why I awoke?' Klingsor, looking out from his tower towards the approaching Parsifal, continues in the same vein: 'Oh how handsome he is, the boy!' Kundry, bowed in sorrow, murmurs 'Must I? Must?'

Klingsor delightedly describes Parsifal as he cuts his way through the shield of enfeebled knights, gathering to defend their beautiful houris from the intruder (29B). Kundry falls into wild hysterical laughter, which gives way to a woeful moan, as Klingsor in demonic mood describes the triumph of Parsifal, proudly standing on the rampart, flushed with victory and laughing with childish surprise. The blue light has dwindled, the stage has darkened and only the sky above the walls is lit. Klingsor turns to summon Kundry, but does not find her, 'Ha! At work already?' he cries. 'Well I know the spell that compels you to serve my aims!' He turns back to Parsifal, saying that the boy will soon be in his power, all purity stripped from him.

The first scene has shown us demonic lust, voyeuristic excitement and sexual slavery, all contained within one of the most abusive relationships ever portrayed on the stage. It ends with a scene-change to match the one that occurred in Act I. The tower rapidly sinks from view, taking Klingsor with it, to be replaced by the magic garden. It is a garden of terraces in Moorish style, with a luxuriant growth of flowers. Parsifal stands on the rampart, gazing in astonishment. The flower-maidens, in light veil-like garments, rush in from every side, as though just startled out of sleep. We are in a world of sensual delight, where desire flits from object to object and no lover is ever more precious than the next one. The object of desire for Klingsor is a thing to be possessed, enslaved, humiliated. The object of desire in the magic garden is a thing to be enjoyed for a while, and then perhaps discarded – or maybe not, it all depends. This theme enters the world of *Parsifal* as a moment of light relief, with music that brilliantly conveys the tangled threads of intrigue, excitement and flirtatious charm.

There is a deeper purpose, too. Often in the late works of Wagner the devices of drama are used to present in immediate and condensed form long processes of moral and psychological change. Such is the drink of forgetting that wipes Brünnhilde from Siegfried's memory; and such is the castle of Klingsor. Parsifal, we are made to understand, is on a journey of discovery: *durch Mitleid wissend*. His path to self-knowledge leads him through places of sensual delight, in which his purity is tested but not lost. Wagner aims to portray sensual delight in all its appeal, showing that it is not *this* that confronts the pure fool with the real existential menace, even if it may also tempt him to drop his guard. We are to imagine a long process of moral development, which opens the way at last to the encounter with Kundry.

The scene opens with a consummate piece of choral writing, using only sopranos, in two groups of three solo voices, above two three-part choirs, each of them divided into two. The effect is of childish bustle and excitement, raised to a way of being. At first the maidens rush around in consternation, seeking their lovers. But Klingsor's knights have taken refuge in the castle, nursing their injuries. The maidens see Parsifal standing triumphant on the battlements, and reproach him for the wounds he has inflicted (30), though with a hint of admiration too. He jumps into the garden, and explains that he was forced to smite their lovers, who had tried to keep him away from these lovely creatures. You knew we were here? they say; you've seen us before? You won't harm us? You'll play with us? You'll seek to console us? And soon they have forgotten their lovers and are competing for the attention of this fascinating intruder. They unite in a waltz (31A) on the words 'Komm'! Komm'! Holder Knabe!' – Come, handsome boy, for you I will blossom, to delight and please you will be my task of love.

How fragrant you are, Parsifal remarks, as they surround him: are you then flowers? Yes, they reply, we must be cherished or we wither and die. They move ever closer, describing in concupiscent accents his physical attractions, and beginning to fight each other for the privilege of being the first to enjoy his love (32). He squirms free of them, half angrily, so that they scatter in fear. He is about to depart when Kundry's voice sounds from the flower-foliage, and he stands still in surprise.

'Parsifal – Stay!'

'Parsifal? So my mother once named me as she dreamed.'

Herzeleide's motif, a highly chromatic, almost atonal melody, effects a total change of atmosphere, from seductive eroticism to remembered love. Kundry, still hidden in the foliage, shoos away the amorous children, telling them to tend to their wounded lovers. The maidens linger, looking regretfully at Parsifal; I would gladly part with my love, each tells him, to be alone with you. Together they sing their farewell:

> Farewell you fair one, you proud one,
> You – fool!

And they run laughing into the castle.

As the prophecy motif (9A) sounds in the orchestra, Parsifal looks around him, searching for the person who called. He wonders whether the garden is a dream, and then catches sight, through an opening in the flower-hedge, of a young and beautiful woman, wearing a light veil-like robe of Arabian style and lying on a couch. 'Did you call to me, the nameless one?' he asks. 'I named you foolish pure one,' she replies, '"Fal parsi", by which your father, Gamuret, in far Arabian lands, called to you, as you stirred in your mother's womb – so he named you as he perished. I waited here to tell you these tidings: what else drew you to me if not the wish to know?'

The phony etymology[12] here should not distract us from the artistic intention, which is once again to underline that no-place named 'Arabia' – the no-place that Kundry intimately knows, and where Parsifal's father, in pursuit of adventure, was lost. This takes up a persistent theme in the Grail literature: the existential divide between Christian and heathen lands, and the need to save what is spiritually pure from the malign force of magic.

Parsifal, whose heart is filled with fear by the sight of Kundry, asks if she is a flower, grown in this lovely garden. You foolish pure one, she replies; my home is far away, though I lingered here so that you would find me. To a new *berceuse*-like theme (33) she recounts how she saw the child on his mother's breast, and heard his childish laughter. This laughter inspired Herzeleide when, through her sorrows, she feasted her eyes on her son. Kundry evokes Herzeleide's mourning for the father whom the boy had lost, her resolution to keep her precious son away from arms and conflict, her anxiety when he roamed late in the forest, her laughter with relief at his return, when she would seize him in her arms – surely he was not afraid of kisses then! But one day the boy did not return; she waited long days and nights and then at last died of a broken heart. The poignant motif of remorse (34), the ambiguous rhythm (is it 9/8 or 3/4?), the sinuous melodic line, all contribute to the seductive power of Kundry's manipulation. Parsifal gives way to grief, accusing himself, blind and blundering fool that he is, of matricide. Through his sorrow, Kundry cunningly suggests, he has earned the right to consolation, and consolation will come from love. To the concluding phrase of the *Grundthema* Parsifal then bewails his own heartlessness and treachery, adding: what else did I forget, what else but folly lives in me? (34, 5B) Once more the dramatic moment summarizes a long process of error and forgetting, the consciousness of which now erupts in Parsifal, in the form of overwhelming remorse.

Kundry's response is that he should acknowledge his fault, and the knowledge will end his folly. Now learn, she adds, about the love of Gamuret for Herzeleide – the love that gave you body and being. From this source I bring to you now, as a mother's last blessing, love's first kiss. And she bends over him to fasten her lips to his.

Kundry is not merely another flower-maiden, tempting her victim to short-term sensory pleasure. One dramatic purpose of the flower-maiden scene is to contrast Kundry's *existential* seductiveness with the flippant and exchangeable delights of the maidens, who have offered Parsifal only a brief apprenticeship in sexual temptation. Kundry steps from the mist of their vagrant pleasures with another goal entirely, which is Parsifal himself, summoned by the name that he has – along with all his mother-need – pushed beneath the threshold of consciousness. She calls to him from a deep pond of desire – desire to confess, to put herself wholly in the other's power, to bring the other's self into the surface of the body where it can be caressed for the precious thing that it is, and to enjoy a like experience herself. Kundry's music makes this abundantly clear – she does not want sensual titillation but substantial union, in which all her longing for acceptance can be fulfilled at the same time and in the same act as her physical passion. Although she is a slave, bound to seduce whomsoever Klingsor has commanded, she withholds nothing from the sexual encounter, wrapping her victim in the chains by which she too is bound. This is the erotic at its most dangerous, and it is why she does her best to fill Parsifal's heart with guilt and longing, so that he will face her as an equal, matching in his excitement the emotions that she wishes to purge. Then, and only then, does she aim to possess him. At the same time, and paradoxically, she sees in Parsifal the chaste man who will resist her, so lifting the curse. She longs for his purity, in order to possess both him and it, and this longing is the source of an irresistible sexual desire – desire for the very thing that desire will destroy.

It is thus that Parsifal, incited to imagine his father's love for Herzeleide, receives from Kundry her soul-shattering kiss. We hear the music of enchantment – the enchantment by which Kundry is imprisoned and which it is her role to propagate. But as before, when Gurnemanz related the fall of Amfortas, the melody lingers at the apex, caught in a semitone lament that also recalls the cry of Amfortas in his agony, before plunging through the wound (4) to a cry of woe (25A). The compassion that Kundry has awoken with the tale of Herzeleide is now fixed on Amfortas, and with sudden insight Parsifal experiences from within the real cause of Amfortas's wound – this desiring, demanding, intoxicating creature that has wrapped her arms around his neck and sucked life from his lips.

The wound that I saw bleeding, Parsifal exclaims, is now bleeding in me, a flame in the heart, a fearful yearning, the torment of love, in which 'alles schauert, bebt und zuckt in sündigem Verlangen' – everything trembles, quakes and quivers in sinful desire.[13] From the depth of his being, accompanied by the Act I Prelude's wonderful synthesis (4, 5A) of the Spear theme and the themes of pain and woe, Parsifal then invokes the Redeemer, remembering the ceremony that he had once witnessed in spellbound silence and the call of the Grail

that sounded in his soul – the call of the holy vessel to be rescued from sin-tainted hands. Not grasping what was then at stake he had fled away, a coward, to wild deeds of childish daring. But now, understanding Kundry's kiss and all that it means, he is overcome with remorse, and begs for absolution. As Wagner put it in the 1865 sketch: 'transferred wholly into the soul of Amfortas, he feels Amfortas' enormous suffering, his dreadful self-reproach; the unspeakable torments of yearning love, the unholy terrors of sinful desire . . . he sees her every gaze, hears her every word, as if from Amfortas' soul . . .'[14]

The great change that comes over Parsifal in the wake of Kundry's kiss is revealed to us in the music. The stage directions tell us that Kundry stares at Parsifal in fear and astonishment, as he falls into a trance. His reference to the torment of love is accompanied by the descending chromatic scale of woe (25A), which sounds twice, each time tailing off with Kundry's scream (11) in its truncated form, coming to rest at last on the triad of E major, pianissimo and with a syncopated pulse. From this, through a succession of magical enharmonic changes, the Grail motif (2) emerges, outlining the object of Parsifal's inner gaze, and leading to the *Grundthema* in its minor version (1A). The bliss of redemption to which Parsifal now refers gives way to the lament of the Saviour (*die Heilands Klage*), in which 25A and 5A are miraculously combined, to give way in turn to a new use of the *Grundthema*, as Parsifal imagines the voice of the Saviour himself, crying 'Redeem me, rescue me from sin-tainted hands':

This passage, the melody, harmony and orchestration of which are closely shadowed in Verdi's contemporary *Otello*, suddenly switches the location of the drama, from the no-place of Kundry's attempted seduction, to the innermost reaches of Parsifal's soul, another no-place which is the true seat of the drama. The *Grundthema*, loaded with prayer, yearning and religious sorrow, has fragmented again, but in a new way, so as to deliver, from the ascending triad of the communion motif, combined with the semitone interval of the wound, the cry of the Redeemer for redemption. The *Qual der Liebe*, the torment of love, has invaded the remembered communion and, as it were, turned the Eucharist against itself. Erotic passion and religious penitence have driven the 'wild childish deeds' from Parsifal's mind, leaving, in the glowing aftermath of their collision, a new sense of what matters in life and why. Parsifal has grasped that it is not Amfortas only who is calling for redemption, but the Redeemer too. In our polluted passions, seeking pleasure and excitement rather than respect and love, we scorn the Redeemer's suffering and surrender to the basest kind of control.

While all this, the music tells us, is going on in Parsifal's soul Kundry is excited to the highest point by his resistance, and renews her advances. As she fondles him, Parsifal imagines the same treatment administered to Amfortas, the same caresses, the same tresses falling across his face, the same arms around his neck, the same longing, the same kiss – and with the thought of her kiss he pushes Kundry away, saying go from me, for ever be gone!

Thus do we see the dawn of understanding in Parsifal – understanding of Kundry's longing in all its many-layered depth and of the transgression to which she is inviting him, the other side of the religious fervour that is distilled in the rising triad of the communion, and also in the rising triad of her enchantment and of the kiss that stems from it. Wagner has united desire and repentance, lust and religious longing, in a musical icon that inextricably mingles the souls of Kundry and Parsifal, as she wrestles to smother him, and he gasps for air. She studies his transports of remorse with growing passion, so that when he finally pushes her away she can only respond with greater vehemence, telling him that she had waited for him, her saviour, for all eternity. She strives to match the call of Amfortas's pain, the music of which she borrows as she confesses to the extraordinary story of her many lives, how she had mocked the Redeemer in his hour of sorrow, and the curse that now torments her, binding her in sleep and waking, driving her onwards through life and death (35). And as she recalls the devastating look with which the Redeemer responded to her mockery we hear the cry of woe in its simplest form, followed by the motif of agony – a musical proof of Kundry's sincerity, and a proof too that all this woe was implanted in the scheme of things long before Amfortas lost and was wounded by the Spear:

She has built her sorrow into her desire, and matched them exactly to what Parsifal is feeling, seriously hoping for the rescue that he can offer, even while deluded into thinking that this rescue will come from the consummation of her ever more urgent physical passion.

In her frenzy she lays bare her soul for Parsifal's compassion, longing for the love that would wipe her agony away. She cannot weep, she says, but only laugh, storm, rage, as another sinner sinks in her arms, and she in turn sinks into the night of her confusion, from which, remorseful, she scarcely wakes. To lie weeping on the breast of the one whom I once despised, she cries, for one brief hour with Him, with you, united, cleansed and redeemed!

It has been left to Kundry to cast Parsifal in the role of Christ, seeing in him the love that 'taketh away the sins of the world', but misconstruing that love as the most intense physical passion. Parsifal therefore rebukes her, saying that, in her arms, forgetful of his calling, he would condemn them both to perdition. There is a fount from which flows a purer grace than that which flows from Kundry's longing. It is for this other grace that he saw the Grail-knights pining, but who knows how to find it in this night of worldly confusion, in which, searching for salvation, we drink from the fount of damnation instead? Parsifal's theological rebuke is less clear in his words than in the music, which vividly contrasts the enchantment of Kundry with the pain and the longing of Monsalvat. But she refuses to accept his version of events, claiming that it was her kiss that enabled him to see things so clearly. Hence the full act of love would raise him to the highest point of understanding, even to the level of a god. Having cast Parsifal in the role of Christ she now casts herself in the role of the serpent in the Garden of Eden, who said 'you shall be as gods'. And if she must pay the price for this, she adds, so be it: let him redeem the world, even if she must be condemned thereby for ever.

Parsifal responds that she can obtain both love and redemption, but not in this way. Let me love you as a god, she says, and I too will be redeemed. Both love and redemption will be yours, he replies, if you show me the way to Amfortas. And at this she bursts into a fury, ridiculing the fallen, shameful Amfortas, the object of her laughter, who fell by his own Spear. And when Parsifal asks who wielded the Spear she replies enigmatically 'He, who once punished my laughter: the curse – ha! it gives me strength.'

To understand this strange remark, in which Kundry seems to identify Klingsor too as a Christ figure, since after all it was Klingsor who wielded the Spear and Christ who punished her laughter, we must recognize that Kundry is treading the thin line between sexual passion and religious awe. Her original vision of the crucified Saviour was the moment when she first stood on that line, defending herself through laughter. And she who mocked is now mocked in her turn. Christ becomes Klingsor, since submission to Klingsor is the price of her sin. Kundry now threatens to summon the Spear against Parsifal too, if he dares to take pity on that sinner Amfortas, for such was the nature of her sin: the refusal to take pity when pity was asked for. In recognition of this she too now pleads for pity: 'Mitleid mit mir!', just one hour of love and I will show you the way to Amfortas! And she throws herself on Parsifal, only to be pushed away – 'Begone, unholy woman!'

What Kundry is demanding from Parsifal is the wrong kind of relation: not the desire that belongs to guilt-free love, that opens the heart to contrition and repentance, but rather the desire that works itself to a climax without offering the real sacrifice on which all love ultimately depends, the sacrifice of self. Kundry's original sin, which was to refuse compassion to the Redeemer in his hour of need, has been punished with a curse that hampers all her ventures into love, replacing the desire to give with an implacable hunger to receive. It is this hunger that Parsifal senses, and which he recoils from, since it is asking him too to be bound by it, to fall away from the world of guilt-free relations, into the black hole where Kundry lingers, abused, guilt-ridden and desperate for love.

We should not see this scene, therefore, simply in terms of a conflict between chastity and desire, as though Kundry were chief whore in Klingsor's brothel. Kundry is not playing with sensual delights, as the flower-maidens are playing. She is not using her allure as an instrument, to turn Parsifal in the direction chosen by Klingsor. She is sincere in her passion; she puts herself wholly on display as a suffering, needy, love-hungry creature, and in this there is a certain nobility to her character (35, 36, 37). Hence, when all her tricks have been exhausted, she can only summon Klingsor's magic, so that all paths from the castle will be barred to Parsifal, and the way to Amfortas will be lost. She curses the boy to wander as she does, with nothing save madness as his guide. Yet, in some secret way, she may also be guiding him, as perhaps she once guided him to Monsalvat.

Klingsor appears on the ramparts, declaring that the fool will fall to his master's Spear. He hurls the Spear at Parsifal, but it remains hanging in the air above the boy's head. Parsifal seizes the Spear and uses it to make the sign of the cross, declaring an end to Klingsor's enchantment. The castle crumbles as though from an earthquake, the garden withers to a desert, the ground is scattered with faded flowers, and Kundry sinks down with a cry. Parsifal hastens to the rampart, where he turns to Kundry, saying 'You know where you can find me again', before vanishing from the scene.

The extraordinary psychodrama of *Parsifal*, Act II, will seem, to a reader of the text, like a series of disconnected traumas. Remorse, grief and desire sweep on to the stage in rapid succession; the longing for purity is eclipsed by the need to destroy it; sexual excitement gives way to immortal longings, which in turn become lust for this mortal body here and now; cries of repentance are quickly succeeded by eager invitations to sin and remembered traumas become implacable demands for sexual pleasure. But all these extremes of feeling are threaded on to the toughest musical cord, which runs unbroken from Kundry's first words to her final cry at the end of the Act. The music weaves together the sacred and the desecrated, the pure and the polluted, the giving and the refusing. We hear the holy as it changes to the unholy and yet remains the same. Such enharmonic changes of the passions, are delivered by the enharmonic language of the score, and the uncanny sense of unity between all that we hope for and all that we fear is in the end what *Parsifal* is about. 'You know where you can find me,' says Parsifal – namely, in you.

Act III opens with a Prelude of unparalleled bleakness, depicting the wandering of Parsifal in search of Monsalvat. Fragments of the *Grundthema* and the prophecy motif emerge above a bass line full of dissonant intervals (39); the strings drag the music upwards against a falling chromatic bass (40); we hear the distorted theme of the Grail cut off by Kundry's scream, and then a vigorous return to the pure fool's intervals of fifth and diminished fifth, with the three-note up-beat of the Spear motif constantly driving the movement towards the bar-line, like someone lost and exhausted who can proceed only by setting himself targets: the next field, the next wall, the next wood, that hill top (41, 42). The result anticipates the sound world of Schoenberg, but the inspiration is Wolfram's image of the Waste Land around the castle of Munsalvaesche: the land that has withered from the wound of the Fisher King.

As explored by Jessie Weston and used by T. S. Eliot, the Waste Land and its Fisher King are familiar to readers of modern literature: residues, according to Weston, of an ancient vegetation cult devoted to the rites of seasonal renewal. In Wagner the Waste Land is displayed first as an inner state, a condition of forlorn self-doubt and isolation, rather than an outward sterility, and this inner desolation, we come to understand, is a necessary stage in the fool's emotional apprenticeship. But as the curtain rises thoughts of sterility are replaced by the sight of a spring landscape within the domain of the Grail. Flowering meadows rise towards the background, and the edge of the forest reaches stage right, where there are a spring and a hermit's hut, built against a mass of rock. Gurnemanz, now very old and grey, dressed as a hermit in the tunic of the Grail knights, steps from the hut and listens.

No wild beast, he reflects, would give out such a woeful moan, and especially not on this most holy morning – indicating with these words that it is Good Friday, the day when, in Wolfram's story, the power of the Grail is renewed, and the day of atonement (46), when the beasts too sense the peace promised by the Redeemer, the peace of man's compassion. Gurnemanz thinks that he recognizes the sound; sure enough, in a thicket of thorns, lies Kundry, cold, stiff and lifeless. (The music here is built from the chromatic theme 38A, used by Kundry in her pleading with Parsifal, giving way to 15, the motif of sorcery.) Gurnemanz drags her from the bushes to a nearby grassy mound, where he rubs her hands and temples, until life returns to her and she opens her eyes with a cry. As in the first Act she wears the coarse robe of a penitent; but the wildness has vanished from her looks and behaviour, and she gazes long at Gurnemanz, before raising herself, arranging her dress and hair and adopting the manner of a serving maid. 'Have you no word for me?' asks Gurnemanz, 'No thanks for awakening you from deathly sleep?', to which the reply is 'Dienen ... dienen' – to serve ... to serve, the only words she utters in Act III – and we hear a brief snatch of the balsam motif (12), the record of her former years as helpmate to the knights of the Grail.

Your task will be light, says Gurnemanz; we send no messages now, and each of us survives by foraging, like the beasts of the forest. As she goes into the hut the old knight reflects on Kundry's changed appearance, and wonders whether she has been sent on this holy day that he might awaken her to salvation. We hear the motif of sorrow, 5B, and then a kind of breath from the meadows, anticipating the Good Friday music, 48. Kundry returns from the hut with a pitcher, and goes to the spring. She notices someone in the distance and, turning, silently draws Gurnemanz's attention to the approaching figure. Peering into the wood Gurnemanz asks himself who it is, approaching the holy spring in gloomy armour – certainly not one of our brothers.

Kundry fills her pitcher and retreats into the hut, as Parsifal enters slowly. He is dressed in black armour, with closed helm and lowered spear, and moves in dreamy uncertainty to the grass mound beside the spring, where he sits. Gurnemanz stares at him in astonishment, and then greets him, offering, if the knight is lost, to give directions. Have you taken a vow of silence, he asks, and is that why you don't reply? In any case, I am bound to tell you plainly that this is a consecrated place, and that no man should bear weapons here, nor a lowered visor, nor a spear. Certainly not today: do you not know what day it is? No? From whence then do you come and among what heathens have you been dwelling, that you do not know that this is the all-holy Good Friday? So saying he commands Parsifal to lay down his weapons, reminding him of the Lord who on this day meekly gave his holy blood in atonement for the sins of the world.

Parsifal raises himself, thrusts the Spear into the ground, lays shield and sword beneath it and, raising his visor, removes his helmet. He kneels before the sacred relic in silent prayer. As he raises his eyes devoutly towards the point of the Spear the orchestra gives out the sorrowful final phrase of the *Grundthema*, and then the whole theme twice over as Gurnemanz ponders first Parsifal, whose identity as the once rejected fool is confirmed by a silent nod from Kundry, and then the Spear, which he greets with great solemnity. Parsifal rises slowly from prayer, looks calmly about him and then, recognizing Gurnemanz, extends a hand in greeting, rejoicing that he is back where he wished to be. Gurnemanz, surprised to be recognized behind the veil of grief and care, asks Parsifal where he has wandered. To the music of the Act III Prelude (40) Parsifal describes the paths of error and suffering that have brought him here; the motif of the breeze from the lake (14), in its diminished form, then supplants that of straying, as Parsifal wonders whether he is right to think that he again greets the good old man he knew before. Or does he err still? For everything seems altered.

Gurnemanz asks Parsifal whom he is seeking, to which the answer is: him whose anguish I once heard in foolish wonder, and to whom I now bring healing (47). Parsifal describes the curse that impeded his journey, and the numberless battles and dangers through which he fought his way to Monsalvat (40, 42). In all his trials, and despite many wounds, he has kept the Spear at his side, unused in battle and therefore un-profaned. Gurnemanz greets this news with transports of joy, the opening phrase of the *Grundthema* now resolved in the motif of redemption (51) and melded to the motif of the angelic gift (17).

Surely, Gurnemanz says, if it was a curse that drove you astray, then the spell is now broken. You stand in the domain of the Grail, where we have need of the healing that you bring. Uniting the opening motif of the Act III Prelude (the motif of desolation, 39) with those expressing the distress of Monsalvat (5B, 6, 43), Gurnemanz recounts how Amfortas, maddened by the pain of his wound, has refused to uncover the Grail, the sight of which would merely keep him alive when what he most wants is to die. Hence the food so bountifully provided by the Grail is no longer available, no supplicants visit Monsalvat, and no calls for help come from distant lands. The knights wander, pale and leaderless, and Titurel, the hero, deprived of the sight of the Grail, has died, human after all.

Parsifal here suffers a crisis of remorse as great, in its way, as the crisis precipitated by Kundry, when she described the lonely death of his mother. Though chosen as a saviour, Parsifal cries, I strayed in wild error, so that the path of salvation was lost to me. And the orchestra makes clear that this, too, reflects his nature as a fool.

On first reflection it may be hard to understand Parsifal's outburst. After all he cannot be blamed for his original ignorance of what was required of him. And when, drawn to Klingsor's castle, the nature of his mission began to dawn on him, it was surely not his fault that he was blind at first to the real meaning of Kundry's enchantment, or to the true cause of Amfortas's wound. If his return to Monsalvat was full of delays, this was because of Kundry's curse. And he incurred this curse by acting rightly towards her, pointing the true way to her salvation at the very moment when her dark side would have damned them both.

However, we should recognize that, in every crucial transition from ignorance to knowledge, we are given two views of Parsifal's predicament: the view from outside, in which he is seen as a creature buffeted by fate, subject to forces that he neither controls nor understands, and the view from inside, his own view, in which he *takes possession* of his destiny, assigns to himself the faults and failings that impede his journey, and strives to see how others suffer because of him. This inward view is not an illusion, but a rival and justified perspective on matters that can be seen in two contrasting ways. It involves a recognition that, in everything that happens to us, there is a choice between the passive view of ourselves as objects driven by fate, and the active adoption of ourselves as subjects, accountable to others, I to thou. It is thanks to Kundry that Parsifal acquired such a response to his mother's sufferings; and it is thanks to Kundry's curse that he has come to see that the world of obstacles is not to be accepted passively but to be confronted and overcome. This growth of the inward view of things is the work of compassion, and it is what is ultimately meant by 'durch Mitleid wissend': the knowledge from within of the other, whose rescue depends on you. But with the growth of compassion comes also desolation, the sense that after all one cannot really get through to the other, cannot reach the source of his feeling, and from that in turn there comes the loneliness so powerfully expressed in the Act III Prelude. I return to this point in Chapter 4, since it lies at the heart of the *Parsifal* philosophy.

Parsifal's experience of the delays and muddles that have kept him from Monsalvat is an experience of error and transgression, and he can experience the effect of Kundry's curse in no other way. His fit of remorse is so great that he is on the point of fainting. Kundry comes forward with a bowl of water to sprinkle him, but Gurnemanz restrains her, as the orchestra softly recalls the moment when Kundry had appealed, in the midst of her frenzied desire, for Parsifal's compassion (37). Gurnemanz insists that the holy spring itself should be used to refresh this pilgrim, who surely has some sacred office to accomplish and must therefore be free from stain. We hear the motif of purity (45) as they move Parsifal to the edge of the spring. Together they relieve him of his armour, as the motif of consecration sounds in the orchestra.

This motif (44) returns us to the idea that is central to Wagner's view of religion, namely that consecration is something that we humans do, without the aid of any supernatural power. We do it when reverence rises within us, to crown the object of our devotion: through touch we then make the thing untouchable, shifting it across the boundary from the secular to the sacred. Parsifal weakly asks whether he will be led to Amfortas this day, and Gurnemanz replies that he surely will, since the castle has been prepared for Titurel's funeral, and Amfortas has sworn, in atonement for his father's death, to perform the sacred office.

Parsifal gazes in wonder at Kundry, who with eager humility is now bathing his feet. Acknowledging her he asks Gurnemanz to bathe his brow, which the old man does by scooping water from the spring. As Gurnemanz blesses Parsifal, the motif of consecration (44) sounds again, Kundry retrieves a golden phial from her tunic and pours the contents over Parsifal's feet, which she then dries with her loosened hair. Parsifal takes the phial from her and passes it to Gurnemanz, asking the old knight, Titurel's companion, to anoint him as king. Here the pleading and yearning motifs, 38, so prominent in Kundry's failed attempt at seduction, return in sweetened form. Throughout the scene of consecration the orchestra weaves the thread of Kundry's former sexual passion into the halo now placed upon Parsifal's head. This mystical union of opposites is the music's doing, and we go along with it without consciously knowing what it means. We are revisiting, in a context of peace and reconciliation, the same interweaving of sin and redemption, pollution and purity, that had taken such an inflamed form in the music of Act II.

Anointing Parsifal, Gurnemanz lays his hands in blessing on the young man's head, describing him as the 'Reiner! Mitleidsvoll Duldender, heiltatvoll Wissender' – the pure one, suffering full of compassion, the knowing one full of healing – who has been redeemed by what he has undergone. The orchestra accompanies him with a symphonic elaboration of the pure fool's consecutive fifths. Unobserved by Gurnemanz, Parsifal leans forward to gather water from the spring, which, to the motif of faith (3), he now pours over the head of Kundry, saying 'Be baptized, and believe in the Redeemer.' Kundry bows her head and seems to weep passionately, to the motif of suffering (6). As Parsifal turns to look ecstatically at the fields and forest, now glowing in the morning light, we hear another breath of the Good Friday music (48). Parsifal recalls the magic flowers that he has seen, which sought to twine themselves around him, but never has he been granted a vision so mild and fair as these meadows with the sweet scent and fresh colours of childhood.

Gurnemanz explains that this is Good Friday magic, at which Parsifal, with a new and expressive use of the *Grundthema*, exclaims against the day of agony, when all living things should only grieve and weep. Gurnemanz replies 'You see that it is not so', and the Good Friday music translates those words into melody. This is the day bedecked with flowers, watered by the tears of repentant sinners, when all creatures rejoice in the holy trace of the Redeemer and raise their prayer to him. We know the Saviour on the cross as other creatures do not, but we pass our redemption to the beasts and the flowers in the form of compassion; they know that on this day the foot of man will tread lightly on the earth. For this is the day when all that blooms and fades is renewed.

Kundry has raised her head and now gazes with tearful eyes at Parsifal, filled with calm and earnest entreaty. To the chromatic motif (38) of the seduction scene Parsifal recalls the flowers that withered when once they laughed at him: they too are yearning for redemption. In this way he evokes Kundry's original transgression, the laughter at the suffering Redeemer, which has been the source of all her woe. You weep for sorrow, he says to Kundry, but look: the meadows are smiling! And he kisses her brow. Nothing has been said to identify Kundry in Parsifal's mind with the seductress of Klingsor's castle; but the music of this scene takes us back to that previous encounter, and suggests that, after all, Parsifal and Kundry in some way know each other completely and that the fractured parts of Kundry's soul are united in Parsifal's forgiving gaze. What began as seduction has ended in baptism, and throughout this strangest of transformations her eyes and feelings have been directed to Parsifal, the unchanging object of her changing desires. Again we encounter a union of opposites, and the chromatic motif 38 perfectly encapsulates this, its two voices moving towards each other in opposite directions, and coinciding at the octave halfway. There is no need to think that either Kundry or Parsifal is aware of the magical change to which they are subjected. As the great American novelist Willa Cather once put it, in 'Three American Singers': 'who can say what memories of Klingsor's garden are left on the renunciatory hands that wash Parsifal's feet?'

In the Good Friday scene something has become clear that has been implied throughout the drama, namely that none of what we have witnessed has taken place in ordinary time. It has often been remarked that holy days have a peculiar atmosphere, a kind of freshness, as though you awake on those days in another world, and look on your fellows with a more than human kindness: this we witness in all that Gurnemanz has said and done since the beginning of Act III. Even if you think, as an observing anthropologist, that this effect is merely a product of human suggestibility, it is familiar to all of us, and recorded in literature down the ages – the *Thesmophoriazusae* of

Aristophanes, the silver Latin *Pervigilium Veneris*, Milton's 'Hymn on the Morning of Christ's Nativity', and a thousand other instances, not least Wagner's great invocation of the Feast of St John in *Die Meistersinger*. Such works address some version of the profound question that Jews ask at the Seder, when making themselves part of the eternal story of their faith: 'Why is this night different from all other nights?' The true explanation of the holy day is that it is a dramatization of the timeless. It is an attempt to represent the endless renewal of things, and the atonement that cleanses us of sin so that we too can begin again. The Jewish holidays are the perfect illustration of this, and one in particular, *Yom Kippur*, the Day of Atonement, is a meditation on repentance and forgiveness comparable to that attached by Gurnemanz to Good Friday. What we experience in the music of this scene is the joy of confession, and the trust in forgiveness and renewal. If there is an expression in music of God's Grace, this, surely, is it.

In the distance the temple bells are sounding, and the theme of the funeral march (50) begins in the orchestra. It is midday, Gurnemanz says. Allow me, your vassal, to lead you. Parsifal takes the Spear, with a solemn gesture, and, with Kundry beside him, follows Gurnemanz. The stage is transformed as in Act I, but in the reverse direction. The three disappear, the forest retreats and the rocks approach, opening at last to show the lofty hall of the Grail temple, without the feast tables of Act I. From one side appear knights bearing Titurel's coffin, from the other side those escorting Amfortas in his litter, preceded by the covered shrine of the Grail. Over the magnificent funeral march the two groups, like a divided chorus in Greek tragedy, engage in a question-and-answer dialogue, the goal of which is a biting accusation aimed at Amfortas:

> While we escort the Grail to the altar, whom do you, in mourning, bear? The hero, Titurel. By whom was he killed? By Age, when he no longer saw the Grail. Who kept him from the Grail? The one you are escorting, the Grail's sinful guardian. We escort him today so that once more he will perform his office, for the last time.
>
> Woe! Woe! For the last time, Guardian of the Grail, perform your office!

This unforgiving assault is conveyed to the highest pitch of sorrow and anger by the extraordinary music, in which the motif of desolation, 39, comes to the fore, sounding above the deep bass bells of the temple – the cry of a community betrayed. Amfortas wearily raises himself, joins in the cry of woe, and begs for death as a small atonement for his sin. Titurel's coffin is opened, to a loud cry of lamentation from the assembled knights. In a haunting passage, using the motif of the angelic gift (17) to slide from triad to triad as though reaching in vain for relief, Amfortas adds his prayer: Father, pure one to whom the angels once came down, who now looks on the Redeemer's face – beseech Him that this life-renewing blood, which is to flow again today, bring death to your son! Two new motifs accompany this passage, one (53) borrowing the rhythm of the angelic bequest, the other (54) a sparse and, as it were, exhausted version of Parsifal's mother-guilt (34). These desolate themes, harmonized with the same chromatic extremism as the theme of desolation (39), show Amfortas reduced to total ruin by his remorse and suffering, and now on the edge of suicide.

As though eager to tip him over that edge the knights crowd around him, ordering him to reveal the Grail: your father demands it; you must! You must! At this, Amfortas springs up in maddened despair and rushes among them, the orchestra accompanying his cries with variants of the original theme of his suffering (8, 52). He tears open his robe, exposing the wound, crying to them to plunge every sword blade deep in his heart, to slay the sinner before them, so that once again the Grail may glow. All shrink away as Amfortas stands alone in a terrible ecstasy. Parsifal, who, with Kundry and Gurnemanz, has appeared among the knights unobserved, now steps forward with the Spear, and touches with its point the wound in Amfortas's side. Amfortas's face shines with holy rapture and, by a tiny but magical adjustment to the original motif of Amfortas's pain (8), the orchestra glows with relief. Amfortas staggers, Gurnemanz reaches out to support him, and what the eyes see as healing, the ears hear as the redemption of Monsalvat.

Be healed, forgiven and atoned, Parsifal says; I shall assume your office. He calls down a blessing on Amfortas's suffering, which brought compassion and wisdom to this reluctant fool. And he raises the Spear high before them all – the weapon that has healed the wound of Amfortas, on the point of which fresh blood is flowing, yearning to join the fountain in the Grail. He orders the squires to open the shrine, ascends the altar steps to take the chalice and sinks to his knees in silent prayer before it. The Grail softly shines as the light above increases. From the height of the dome the choir of boys, youths and knights sings 'Highest holy wonder: redemption to the Redeemer', and a dove descends to hover over Parsifal's head. Kundry, her gaze lifted to Parsifal, sinks down dead (according to the stage directions *entseelt*, de-souled); Amfortas and Gurnemanz kneel in prayer before him, as he waves the Grail in blessing above them all.

So ends, in an atmosphere variously described as provocative, holy, religiose and blasphemous,[15] the story of Parsifal's quest – not for the Grail only, but for the healing of Amfortas, the restoration of the Grail community and the redemption of Kundry in death.

3

Confronting the Enigma

Parsifal is a drama of things suffered more than things done, even if some of these things – Amfortas's agony, Klingsor's enslavement of Kundry, Kundry's attempted seduction of Parsifal – involve the utmost agitation and emotional violence. The conclusion of the work, in Wagner's stage directions, appropriates the icons of the Christian faith without the slightest diffidence, placing Parsifal at the centre of the well-known and deeply emotional rituals of Holy Communion, with a dove hovering above him as though returning him to his eternal place in the Holy Trinity. (In Wolfram, a dove descends every Good Friday to deliver the host to the Grail, so renewing its power; but this excuse for the dove is not mentioned in Wagner's stage directions.) Those present at the early performances, during the period when Cosima managed (as Wagner had wished) to confine performances of *Parsifal* to Bayreuth, testify to the shattering effect of this conclusion on the audience, most of whom at that time would have been familiar with Holy Communion as a religious rite. Many were reduced to tears by the sight of Parsifal standing as though transfigured, bathed in cascades of A flat major as the motif of faith rained from above, and all left the theatre speechless and overwhelmed. But who could say what it meant?

In Christian teaching compassion must be pursued with humility if it is to be a true spiritual resource. It is of course not appropriate for the hero to heal the wound, return the Spear, and then sit down with a 'don't mention it'. The blessing that he brings to the community he must also receive from it, and indeed from the Grail itself. But then it is the Grail, not its newly anointed king, that is the focus of adoration, and the king would more clearly prove his worthiness to be anointed by retreating into the background, and melding into the community that his actions have saved. As it is, Parsifal's command to Gurnemanz to anoint him as king, followed by his taking posses-sion of the ceremony, recall the gesture of Napoleon, as he took the imperial crown from Pope Pius VII, and placed it on his own head.

This seizure of control reflects sentiments already present in the Eucharist, in Wagner's version. The striding, manly theme of the love-feast (28), and the words and music of the invitation to com-munion (27), focus on the strength, pride and bravery produced in the communicant by the body and blood of the Saviour, which become, through their consumption at communion, the body and blood of his soldiers. By contrast, the Eucharist in the Christian Churches is con-ceived as a humble and contrite petition, and has none of this military bravura. Both Roman Catholic and Protestant versions take us back to a vital passage in the New Testament: the humble words precisely of a military man (a centurion) in Matthew 8:8: 'Lord, I am not wor-thy that thou shouldest come under my roof: but speak the word only, and my servant shall be healed.' This becomes the prayer before communion in the Roman Catholic Mass, which in the Tridentine version reads: *Domine, non sum dignus, ut intres sub tectum meum: sed tantum dic verbo, et sanabitur anima mea* – Lord, I am not worthy that thou shouldest come under my roof, but speak the word only, and my soul shall be healed. The Anglican Book of Common Prayer, taking in another image from the New Testament (Mark 7:28), together with a pertinent theological coda from 1 John 14:16, goes a stage further, with the Prayer of Humble Access, which reads thus in the version of 1662:

> We do not presume to come to this thy Table, O merciful Lord, trust-ing in our own righteousness, but in thy manifold and great mercies. We are not worthy so much as to gather up the crumbs under thy Table. But thou art the same Lord, whose property is always to have mercy: Grant us therefore, gracious Lord, so to eat the flesh of thy dear Son Jesus Christ, and to drink his blood, that our sinful bodies may be made clean by his body, and our souls washed through his most precious blood, and that we may evermore dwell in him, and he in us. Amen.

Without making too great an issue of the difference here, we must at least acknowledge that the aspect of Christianity that most offended Nietzsche – the aspect of humility, meekness and self-deprecation – has been marginalized in Wagner's version, and what remains is all the more enigmatic for this, since – unlike the Christian liturgies – the Eucharist at Monsalvat does not put our salvation within reach of our prayers. Indeed one might conclude that the ceremony with which the drama ends is not a celebration of the Eucharist at all, but a kind of anthropologist's caricature. The scene inevitably pushes the producer down the path that has proved so disastrous to Wagner's legacy, and so painful to all true lovers of his art: the path of *Regietheater*, in which staging, costumes, setting and even plot are rewritten according to the clever ideas of the producer, whose ego stands between the audience and the drama, moving in time to the music like a puppet bouncing from the pit.

Striking in this connection has been the celebrated 2008 production for the Bayreuth Festival by Stefan Herheim, who – like so many German producers – believes that justice can be done to a Wagner music-drama only if the tragedy of twentieth-century Germany is rehearsed in the course of it. Act I is set in the Wagner household of Wahnfried during the Second Reich. In an adaptation of the plot inspired by the fighting words of Wagner's communion service, Herheim sends the knights of Monsalvat marching off at the end of Act I into the trenches of the First World War. Klingsor's flower-maidens become the nurses in a field hospital, and, after Parsifal has copulated with Kundry in a field tent, a striking *coup de théâtre* brings stormtroopers swarming across the ruins of what has by now become the starving Weimar Republic. Continuing the history lesson into the last Act requires considerable ingenuity, as we hurry to an ambiguous future beyond the spat-upon Bundesrepublik. But there is neither triumph nor transcendence at the end. Parsifal disappears, and Gurnemanz and Kundry remain, she staying alive in A flat major despite being doused with that cold A minor shower. And with them is an unexplained child, who may or may not be the next in the line of disappointing redeemers.[1]

Dimitry Tcherniakov, in his production for the Berliner Staatsoper, goes one stage further, so as to strike at the very core of Wagner's drama by making sexual passion into its central theme. *Parsifal* becomes the story of the love between Amfortas and Kundry, both of them prisoners of a community of religious maniacs under the puritanical tyrant Gurnemanz. The maniacs get their kicks from drinking Amfortas's blood, which they drain from the wound of their agonized human milch cow. Parsifal's mission is to overcome the superstition that requires this cruel procedure, and which impedes the mutual passion of Amfortas and Kundry. In the climax of Act III Parsifal, having led Amfortas and Kundry to each other so that they can snog in A flat major, sinks into the background, a smiling voyeur. The scene ends when the incensed Gurnemanz, to the relief of every decent Wagnerian in the audience, plunges a knife into Kundry's back.[2]

Even if we deplore such mutilations of Wagner's masterpiece, it is hard to envisage a straight version of *Parsifal*, in which the composer's stage directions prevail. Regardless of the overweening holiness of *Parsifal*, modern producers tend in any case to the view that Wagner's miracle-ridden scenarios are tainted with melodrama and blown up to excess. Adorno called them 'phantasmagoria', in which petty emotions acquire heroic shapes, lifted into legendary landscapes where they can strut in borrowed costumes and look down from an infinite height on the real human world.[3] For many critics the Wagnerian stage heralds the blockbuster movie, in which effects exist without causes, and the thin, slack action is pumped up by music until taking off like a swollen balloon above the empty landscape of the plot.

The history of Wagnerism does nothing to undermine that response, and indeed partly explains the movement launched at Bayreuth by Wieland Wagner's 1951 production, which preferred abstract sets and timeless, placeless costumes to the full paraphernalia of legend. Wieland was aware, however, that abstraction is not enough, and that the drama must be attached to something that we know and towards which we can orient our attention if it is to make sense to us. Symbolism in the theatre is all very well; but symbols are meaningful only if they are also real and living elements of the drama.

There is no doubt that *Parsifal* poses large questions of interpretation that no producer can avoid. The story brings into relation four highly ambiguous, not to say uncanny, characters – Parsifal, Kundry, Klingsor and Amfortas – along with the innocent narrator,

Gurnemanz, who plays a role comparable to that of the Evangelist in the Bach Passions, a comparison that Wagner surely intended. The circumstances that bring these characters together are not accidental, but reflect what is deepest in all of them. And this is the Grail's doing. Reaching into the world of contingencies from the serene sphere whence it came, the Grail calls to its service those mortals who, through their example and their suffering, can show what the life of discipleship means. Underpinning the narrative is the idea of a 'calling', a summons to each of us that will not be denied. The 'calling' is the existential challenge, to *become what you are*, though not in the sense given to that phrase by Nietzsche, who intended a radical individualism that defied old-fashioned norms, on the way to a new and undeceived morality. In *Parsifal* disobedience to the call is certainly an existential fault; but it is a fault exhibited in one's relationship to others. It is a fall from purity to pollution, so as to become the *wrong kind of thing*, related to others in *the wrong kind of way*.

In traditional Christianity the communion ritual, which re-enacts the Redeemer's supreme gift of atonement, results in an 'at-one-ness' that 'taketh away the sins of the world'.[4] But this idea depends on a truth that is downplayed in Wagner's liturgy: the truth that forgiveness cannot be assumed, and comes only through humility, confession and judgement. One of the many puzzles presented by *Parsifal* lies here: what is meant by redemption, when judgement and reward have no real part in it? To answer that question we must explore the deep questions of philosophical anthropology raised by Wagner's drama, and also resist the temptation to interpret the opera in such a way that the question does not arise.

Parsifal is replete with psychological symbols, many of them rooted in the Grail legend itself. The father who commands from the tomb, compelling his son to undergo excruciating torment in atonement for a sexual transgression; the seductive woman who elides into the buried mother, and then begins her seduction with a maternal kiss; the wound that is healed only by the weapon that caused it, and only when Spear and chalice are united; the sacrificial victim, whose blood nourishes the community of love – at every point the story suggests themes from Freud, Jung, Melanie Klein, René Girard and many more. And the immense cruelty of the sufferings depicted – Kundry's curse and enslavement, Amfortas's excruciating wound, Klingsor's tormented self-destruction, even Parsifal's remorseful and bewildered wanderings – point to a world that makes no place for the doctrine of an all-wise and benevolent creator. The rejection of that doctrine is already implied in Wagner's idea of a Redeemer who has gone from the world, leaving only mysterious traces in his wake.

Although Wagner could not have read Sir James Frazer's *The Golden Bough*, the first edition of which appeared in 1890, seven years after the composer's death, Wagner's writings on religion anticipate the central thesis of that book. Ethnographers had assumed that rituals owe their meaning to the myths that they summarize. In fact, Frazer argued, it is the other way round: the myths are to be explained by the rituals. The central fact in any religion is the ceremony: the sacred moment whose inner meaning cannot be stated in prose. Myths are commentaries on these sacred moments, attempts to rationalize them by providing a narrative into which they are subsumed, as the ritual of Holy Communion is subsumed in the story of Christ's Passion.

Wagner brought a similar conception to his understanding of the Grail legend. There is a mystery in the heart of this story, he perceived, and the mystery does not reside in the many puzzling things that Chrétien de Troyes and Wolfram von Eschenbach describe, but in the thing that they do not describe, which is the ritual of the Christian religion – the thing of which all their characters are aware, but which none of them refers to. That ritual stands at the centre of *Parsifal*, and although a few hints are offered as to its explanation, they are of less dramatic significance than the ritual itself, conceived as the re-enactment of an original sacrifice, which must be repeated for ever, regardless of the cost.

In a series of works written in the first decades of the twentieth century, in which both Wagner and Frazer loom large, Jessie Weston argued that the Perceval epics were offshoots of ancient vegetation cults, whose primary meaning was the cycle of nature, the death of the old year and the birth of the new. She focused on the 'Fisher King' and the Waste Land around the castle of the Grail. The hero must heal the Fisher King so that the land can flower and the cycle of nature resume. Although Chrétien de Troyes avoids any suggestion that the king has been wounded in his sexual parts, the suggestion is clearly present in Wolfram, reinforcing Weston's belief that the story derives from a fertility cult, in which the reproductive power of the god is the real topic of the mystery: the Fisher King must become fertile again, so that the waters may flow and the land may bloom, bearing fruit with new seed.[5]

Seen in this way, as a story constructed from the images and rites of a mystery cult, the symbols begin to fall into place, as do their wider implications for the world that we know. For Weston the Bleeding Lance borne by a squire and the Grail carried by a maiden (details that occur in both Chrétien's and Wolfram's versions of the story) were sexual emblems in an ancient vegetation rite. The Grail stories, she argued, arose from the attempt both to invoke that ancient rite, and also to conceal it from the eye of the Church, which was originally closely associated with the mystery cults of antiquity. 'Between these Mystery cults and Christianity,' she wrote, 'there existed at one time a close and intimate union, such a union as of itself involved the practical assimilation of the central rite, in each case a "Eucharistic" Feast, in which the worshippers partook of the Food of Life from the sacred vessels.'[6]

Weston discovered references to the mystery cults in the Tarot cards, and connected both the cards and the Grail to the dying and reborn gods assembled by Frazer. Her work influenced the title, the notes and the imagery of T. S. Eliot's *The Waste Land* – though the poet later disingenuously dismissed the notes as unimportant, designed merely to fill the pages of the book. Building on Weston, Frazer, Jung, Eliade and many more in his monumental summary of the world's mythologies, Joseph Campbell argued that 'the Castle of the Grail, like the bowl of a baptismal font or the sanctuary of the winged serpent, is the place – the *vas*, the *temenos* – of regeneration and, as such, a sanctuary in which sexual symbolism is both appropriate and inevitable.'[7]

My own view is that we should be suspicious of this approach, which offers a wealth of analogical reasoning without the psychic root that would explain it. Sequences of the kind spear = phallus = manhood = quest, or hanged-man = Odin = Attis = Christ, will not

lead us to the 'concealed deep truths' within religion as Wagner conceived it. The real question remains: what have these symbols to do
with religion, with that hunger for membership, for cleansing and
for the overcoming of primordial guilt which overflows in ritual and
in the encounter with sacred and forbidden things? Moreover, however we answer those anthropological questions, Frazerean analysis
of Weston's kind stops short of aesthetic judgement. It makes no
discrimination between the potent and the impotent symbol,
between the image that enters the soul with a shock of recognition,
and the lazy reproduction of a stock effect. Wolfram's references to
the Waste Land around Munsalvaesche are certainly of great anthropological interest. But they hardly compare with the desolate Prelude
to Act III of *Parsifal*, or to the poem that T. S. Eliot composed on the
same idea. In these latter works we are being acquainted with something in ourselves which, but for the work of art, we might never
have recognized. We are being made to visit the desolation that we
carry in our hearts, and which is always there until we resolve to
confront it.

Of course, it is undeniable that the story of Parsifal is to be located
in the emotional field indicated by Weston and Campbell. It concerns
the decay and regeneration of a community, the opposition between
the compassion that renews the world, and the power-hunger that
exhausts it. It touches on the mysterious longing for purity in all of
us, and the defilement that can occur through sexual domination and
abuse. These are themes that we encounter in Jung's well-known
studies of mythological and alchemical symbols, and it is no surprise
that the Grail legend has been the subject of a full-scale Jungian
commentary from Emma Jung,[8] who draws on her husband's studies
of alchemy to unmask the meaning for all of us of the abandoned
mother, the girl by the wayside with her dead lover in her arms
(a theme from Wolfram), the unasked question that might have healed
the wound, and the holy vessel containing the blood of life. In this
way the Perceval legend is given an allegorical form, telling just the
same story as the books of alchemy, and as the tales of Oedipus,
Antigone and the rest – the story of the self in its search for the anima
that completes it, healing the wounds of separation from the mother,
so as to become the 'divine son of the mother' as in a *pietà*.

Emma Jung's study sets the tone for those many productions of *Parsifal* that wish to impose a Freudian, Jungian or similarly symbolic interpretation on the drama, showing it to be a portrait of everyman, and so by-passing the specific characters who bear the burden of the action. But symbolism is meaningful only if the drama secures our sympathy, and this it will never do if the symbols are the centres of attention and the characters have disappeared behind them. Indeed, it is precisely because the drama is so rich in symbolic meaning, and so weighted with significances of a universal and trans-historical kind, that the action should be understood as Wagner describes it – as a sequence of concrete events involving real characters, in the medieval setting that reflects their shared beliefs.

Those reservations notwithstanding, it is surely true that the vision of renewal and healing that forms the background to the narrative of *Parsifal* is brought a little nearer to us by Jessie Weston and Joseph Campbell. But to understand this vision in its full moral significance we need to draw on concepts that belong to a wider philosophical anthropology, and which capture more effectively the heart of religion, and its place in the life of its devotees: the concepts of purity, compassion and moral knowledge to which Wagner himself draws attention in the motto of his hero: *durch Mitleid wissend, der reine Tor* – knowing through compassion, the pure fool.

Wagner had been deeply impressed by his reading of the Greek tragedians, and devotes a long passage of *Opera and Drama* to reflections on the Oedipus of Sophocles, anticipating subsequent theories of what anthropologists, following Mary Douglas, call the ethic of pollution and taboo.[9] Oedipus' faults – parricide and incest – were committed unawares. But the stain of them is not removed by this, and indeed spreads from Oedipus to the city. Thebes is contaminated by Oedipus' presence, and only if he is cast out will the city be cleansed. Oedipus is polluted because he has crossed a boundary, from the world of ordinary wrongdoing, into the world of forbidden relations. His crime is existential, and therefore not to be expiated by punishment or penitence. He has become the wrong kind of thing, and his presence in the city pollutes its moral foundations.

For the Greeks, breaches of sexual taboos and family pieties were not the only, or even the primary, forms of pollution. The defiling of a religious sanctuary was an equally serious fault, and again was not mitigated by the fact that it was committed unawares. In Sophocles' tragedy of Philoctetes the hero makes the mistake of walking on sacred ground on the island of Chryse, for which fault he is bitten in the foot by a snake. The wound causes great pain and does not heal, emitting a dreadful odour that causes Philoctetes' fellow warriors to cast him ashore on the desert island of Lemnos. Wagner was clearly influenced by this story in devising the character of Amfortas, who has defiled a religious sanctuary and as a result obtained an agonizing wound that will never heal, until touched again by the weapon that caused it. Interestingly, though, Wagner mixes the desecration of the sanctuary, through the loss and pollution of its relics, with the sexual transgression that is the root cause of the loss.

To the modern secular mind the ethic of pollution and taboo cannot fail to seem quaint and superstitious, a vestige of tribal ways of thinking which it is our duty, in our complex, rule-governed and contractual world, to put behind us. On the other hand this ethic touches on deep truths about our social nature, and these truths were vital to Wagner, who looked for the existential predicaments rather than the accidental circumstances of his characters. We can see this most clearly when it comes to sexual conduct. A crude caricature of the liberal morality tells us that sexual relations, like other relations, should be governed by the doctrine of consent. If each party freely consents to what the other does, then there are no grounds for an adverse judgement. Ideas of desecration and pollution add nothing of moral significance; and the suggestion that we should fence the sexual act around with a wall of shame belongs to another and antiquated era.

But it is surely obvious that the superficial and perhaps frivolous consent to a particular act does not amount to the real existential yes that opens the door to sexual union. It is therefore possible to consent to what is later understood as a violation and defilement. Hence, as Max Scheler argued in a powerful work, shame emerges spontaneously from the depths of sexual desire, shielding us against acts to which we may have consented with our words, but not with our being.[10] Shame, as he put it, is a *Schutzgefühl*, a shielding emotion, which protects us from the wrong kind of relation. That which is experienced with a brief spasm of pleasure might be later felt as a profound violation. When it comes to understanding rape and sexual abuse such ideas are impossible to avoid. Rape is a pollution of the victim, and it requires no imagination to understand why Lucretia went on to kill herself, whatever physical pleasure she may have felt in the arms of the man whom she briefly mistook for her husband.

The studies of sexual emotion by such phenomenological thinkers as Scheler, Kolnai and von Hildebrand make it abundantly clear that thoughts of pollution and purity are not simply accidental features of sexual activity in its modern context, but an intrinsic part of what is felt, when things go wrong and consent turns to revulsion.[11] Our greatest dramatists, Shakespeare, Racine, Schiller and Wagner pre-eminently, have all been aware of this, and ideas of purity, desecration and shame pervade the treatment of desire and love in all their mature works.[12]

It is important in this context to recognize the duality of human nature. We are animals bound by genetic imperatives, and this may go some way to explaining (though no way to justifying) the incest taboo. But we are also rational beings, accountable to each other for what we are and what we do. When it comes to sexual relations it is less our evolution as animals than our nature as freely choosing persons that is at stake. Conceptions of sexual purity are part of living a free and self-confident life, bound by those I/Thou relations that are essential to our happiness. It is in such terms that we should understand the complex revulsion of Parsifal, when Kundry sought to create in him a change of condition from which there would be no turning back. Kundry, in her role as seductress, is a reworking, in more sophisticated form, of the Venus of *Tannhäuser*. She represents sexual transgression, conceived as an existential fault, a turning towards another way of being, outside the realm of interpersonal fulfilment.

Although Klingsor's castle is a place of illusion it is, in some aspects, a realistic picture of adolescent dreams. Young love contains a large element of self-deception: in our first enthusiasm we conspire with each other to maintain the charm of emotions that do not bear too much scrutiny, and on which only the lightest burden can be reliably placed. Yet, if we retain our self-respect, we can enjoy the delights of such a love without falling into the abyss of self-pity when things are ended, or living thereafter with a sting in the flesh. Wagner's flower-maidens are the musical proof of this – sweet, seductive, dispensable and, once enjoyed, as easily forgotten as recalled. Parsifal, we note, approaches Klingsor's castle with a childish sense of adventure, laughing at the challenge. Condensed into his encounter with the flower-maidens is the story of a boy growing up, learning how to enjoy what is offered as enjoyment, ignorant as yet of his deeper destiny.

Kundry, however, is something else – not a flower but a person, a needy person with a developed and predatory selfhood of her own. What she represents for Parsifal is not sensual pleasure only, but an existential challenge – an entanglement that threatens to deprive him of the purity that excites her. Parsifal confronts our human predicaments with an innocent bewilderment that prevents him from understanding them. He does not want to possess or to dominate, but only to heal, so that, when he does understand, it is not through the attempt to make use of those whom he sees, but through an instinctive movement of sympathy. And this sympathy can be extended even to the woman who lies in wait for him, eager to rob him of the purity that she envies and desires. To get to her he must lift the veil of sexual delights, to encounter what lies behind the enchantment, the thing that addresses him with another, more urgent and more ominous voice: the voice of the self.

Goethe's *Ewig-Weibliche* – woman conceived as a universal principle – has not done any favours to women. Abstracting from the individual and all the contingencies that are the stuff of real love, we easily arrive at ugly stereotypes, although, of course, Goethe's intention was the opposite of this. The image of woman as serpent, whose coiling embrace turns suddenly to a threatening constriction, has been a recurrent theme of our literature and also of medieval iconography, and in a letter to King Ludwig, sent just subsequently to the prose sketch of 31 August 1865, Wagner compares Kundry to the serpent in the Garden of Eden, as I did earlier.[13] Indeed, it is this aspect of Kundry that is foregrounded in the moment of the kiss (16). Her chromatic music slithers towards its target, and the lingering slide between E sharp and F sharp shows this kiss in its true light, as the kiss of Klingsor's creature. This is emphasized by the enharmonic change of E sharp to F, as Parsifal jumps away, the F rewritten in the tonal language of the *Grundthema* so as to announce the motif of pain:

This enharmonic change is a musical refusal, not of love or compassion, but of the hidden goal of Kundry's desire, which is to possess Parsifal in his freedom. It is not sexual pleasure, arrived at by whatever means, that interests Kundry. It is Parsifal himself, whom she desires as a free subject of consciousness. She seeks to possess him as the thing that he is for himself, the pure fool whose purity withstands every effort to grasp and pollute it. She desires both to overcome that purity and to be thwarted in the attempt.

At the same time, because of her imprisoned status, Kundry's desire for Parsifal is in a certain measure unfree, the desire of a puppet, obedient to her master's commands. Hence she threatens to contaminate the object of her desire as Klingsor has contaminated her. Her desire is of a kind that leads of its own accord to abuse, bypassing all the real and respectful paths of freely given love in its pursuit of conquest. The point is that there is an abyss into which we may fall, losing our freedom and self-respect, becoming polluted in our own eyes and in the eyes of our community. The sexual act takes us to the edge of this abyss; only in the context of right relations with the partner can we be sure that we will not fall.

All those thoughts are suggested by the moment of the kiss, and the enharmonic change that accompanies Parsifal's revulsion. This moment takes us back, too, to the original source of Wagner's drama.

Wolfram's *Parzival* presents a society in which mouth-to-mouth kissing is a normal part of courtesy – the way in which a hostess greets her guest or a mother her child. There is no suggestion that this need be other than good manners when it is practised outside the family circle. But it is also clear that the girls in Wolfram's story, when a visiting knight arouses their interest, do not withhold this courtesy, and sometimes crawl into the visitor's bed to administer it. This is Wagner's cue for the kiss of Kundry – the kiss that begins in transferred mother love, compassion and confession, to become a kiss of sexual excitement.

I am reminded of the great passage devoted to sexual desire in Sartre's *L'Être et le néant*.[14] In my normal dealings with other people, Sartre argues, the other comes before me as a 'for-itself', and the look that I direct towards him targets a self-conscious being, who stands to his body in a relation of 'transcendence'. My look seeks the horizon from which the other addresses me, the revelation in the world of objects of a freedom other than my own. In desire this revelation of the other takes on a new character. Desire, Sartre argues, is not desire for the sexual act or for sexual pleasure: it is desire for the other *in his freedom*. The other's look 'fashions' my body: it shapes me as another transcendence, a subjectivity revealed in the world of objects. In this sense the other holds the secret of what I am: he looks at the thing that I can never see, the self, incarnated in the flesh by the other's gaze. In the trouble of my desire, the other is the target of an impossible demand, which is my demand that I possess his body as he himself possesses it, through the fact that it is *his*, the incarnation of a subjectivity that he alone enjoys. The caress of desire is therefore not merely contact with the other's flesh; it is a shaping of the flesh, so as to outline the subjectivity that lies otherwise hidden within. Through the caress I strive to realize the incarnation of the other and at the same time to reveal my own incarnation as the target of his interest. In such a way 'desire is the desire to appropriate the Other's incarnated consciousness'.[15] While desire expresses itself in the conjunction of bodies, it is not the bodies that are desired, but the bodies as expressing and revealing 'transcendence': the horizon of the 'I'. Desire is therefore inherently compromising, placing the free subjectivity in ambiguous relation to the other, as something that might at any moment 'over-step the mark'. Desire exists on the boundary between existential transgression and purity of heart, or – to put it in Wagnerian terms – between sin and salvation.

Hence kisses and caresses, when born from desire, have a quite different intentionality from the kisses and caresses of normal affection and friendship. The caress and kiss of friendship might be physically indistinguishable from the caress and kiss of desire; but the first reassures, the second *explores*. In the kiss of desire the 'I' is called into the lips: when kissing you in this way it is you, the I that you are to yourself, that I kiss; I want you to kiss me in the same way, and I want these reciprocal desires to show themselves in the flesh, to be there *in* the lips. The kiss of friendship, courtesy or mother love has quite another intentionality – that is to say, another form of 'direction' on the world.[16] It does not focus on the lips or even on the act of kissing; it is a gesture of reassurance, whose meaning lies elsewhere. In the erotic kiss the meaning of the kiss lies in the kiss, the I-to-I encounter that is distilled into the mingling of flesh. The kiss of vicarious motherhood that Kundry plants on the mouth of Parsifal might undergo no physical change when it becomes the kiss of passion; but it must undergo a change of focus, a change of *intentionality*. It is this change of intentionality that sparks off the sudden revulsion in Parsifal.

The kiss is the thin edge between consolation and transgression – as it were, the line between E sharp and F, in the crucial passage (16). The kiss can seal the bond of love, or it can push through the barrier of freedom so as to reach for the other's subjective being. Moreover the kiss takes on yet another character in the context of seduction. As Sartre argues, seduction changes the way in which the parties perceive each other.[17] As seducer I put myself unguarded in the field of another's attention. I seek to overwhelm him with the plenitude of my being, to come before him as the thing that will compensate for whatever he might lose through giving way to me. He is to become conscious of his nothingness, in order to surrender precisely that – the nothingness at the heart of his being which is what his consciousness ultimately is. Seducers therefore endanger themselves: they drop their guard in the face of the other's look. In inviting surrender they surrender in turn, and expose themselves to a radical rejection: rejection of what they are. So Kundry appears to Parsifal. In recoiling from her kiss he is recoiling from the chaos that drives her, the hunger that cannot be satisfied since it is the hunger to be something other than what she is.

In Wagner's drama, therefore, the kiss becomes a symbol and an instance of the precarious balance of the human condition. The purpose is not to reject sexual desire, or to portray it as the source of evil. Wagner was first among composers to explore the exaltation that resides in sexual feeling: and in *Tristan und Isolde* he even conceives desire, in its purely personal form, as a kind of redemption, though a redemption in death. But in the moment of desire the free being is overcome by the flesh, and this 'overcoming' of our higher aims and aspirations poses a potential threat to our integrity. In this sense true desire, desire for the other as a free subjectivity, is always also an existential crisis.

In the chromaticism of *Tristan und Isolde* we hear desire, born from the look of love, as it entwines two honest people together and leads them to destruction. The lovers are seized by a force that arises within them, but which grips them as though from outside. Tristan and Isolde willingly accept the death that beckons, and which stares at them already in that first look of love. And the magic enshrined in the music is their doing – they have not fallen into some alien world, ruled by an evil magician. They are simply acting out, in the daylight reality, the inner imperative that binds them to each other and to the night.

That is one reason why the chromaticism of *Tristan* is so different from that of *Parsifal*. As I discuss in Chapter 5, the chromatic harmonies in *Tristan* issue from the contrapuntal treatment of consecutive semitones. The effect is of voices weaving around each other in close harmony: the magic is the result of mutual attraction, like the love between the protagonists, and if we can speak of spells here they are *human* spells, to which the parties willingly submit since they cast them on each other in their shared excitement.

In *Parsifal*, however, we enter a world in which magic is an outside force, a kind of un-creation of the created world, used by the magician to gain power over others. Klingsor's magic is an undoing of the world, and is used always *against* the one on whom it is practised.

The chromatic themes around Kundry and Klingsor do not have the aura of human tenderness that attaches to the leading motifs of *Tristan*. They are coiling, mesmerizing themes, targeting the thing on which they prey. And the sound world of Monsalvat is radically different in yet another way, offering shifting cushions of triadic harmony which offer only temporary and uncertain relief.

Just how Kundry and Klingsor became acquainted we do not know. Kundry is denounced as a sorceress by the squires in Act I, and the intimate antagonism between her and Klingsor has a decidedly marital character. Maybe, before his act of self-mutilation, Klingsor was Kundry's lover: maybe it was she who caused him to wreak this violence on himself. Whatever the truth of the matter, Klingsor acquired, through his mutilation, initiation into black arts, along with a devilish hatred of others and their normal joys. And by means of the black arts he has bound Kundry in the most abusive of all sexual relations – one in which she is compelled not only to seduce whom he wills, but also to undergo the degradation of an unwanted but also craved and no-holds-barred encounter. Meanwhile Klingsor watches, anticipating with obscene excitement the moment when he can enjoy the sexual triumph of his slave. He is a voyeur whose greatest delight is to create shame and self-disgust in the puppet who works his will.

It is this world of sexual abuse, forced relations and the destruction of inner freedom that Klingsor has conjured into his castle, and it is from this world that Parsifal recoils, when he understands the meaning of the kiss – the kiss that brings with it the *Qual der Liebe*, the torment of erotic love, that can sweep a person into the polluted relations that destroyed Amfortas.

It is in something like that way, I believe, that we should understand the ideas of purity and sin implied in the calling of *der reine Tor*. Of course, the medieval setting of the drama makes it plausible to conceive purity simply as chastity, and pollution simply as the loss of it, as the knights of the Grail lose their chastity in the arms of the flower-maidens. But, while that idea of purity is plausible in the context of the original story, it fades beside the more potent idea that Wagner uses it to express – the far-reaching pollution of a person's freedom and being, when treated as an object of sexual domination. This, for a self-conscious being, is the paradigm of moral pollution, and a root cause both of the loss of individual self-respect and the dissolution of communities. Mary Douglas was surely right to argue, in *Purity and Danger*, that the fear of pollution stands watch over those dangerous places where the wrong action, however undertaken, can point a community towards its ruin.

Some things can be given without being lost: love, for example. To want another's love is to want something that he can give, and in the normal circumstances he will gain from giving it. Things are otherwise with purity. Purity given away is purity lost. And to want another's purity is to want what cannot be gained. This is Kundry's case, and explains why her desire for Parsifal aims at an act of existential appropriation, a seizing of the other without regard for what he might thereby become.

However, that is not the whole story. The kiss that condemns Kundry in Parsifal's eyes is also a bid for rescue. Although Kundry is tempting Parsifal towards a contaminated love, one that will undermine his nature as the pure fool, she is hoping to rid herself of an equal contamination. In the dialogue that follows, which is one of Wagner's dramatic triumphs, we encounter the truth of Kundry. Her sexual hunger arises from the hope that she might expiate a primal fault. Kundry is a woman with a past, and Wagner brings together the Hindu doctrine of reincarnation and the legend of Ahasuerus, the Wandering Jew, in a bold but convincing dramatization of the way in which someone can be enslaved by actions that nothing now can remedy. She lives in hiding from herself, longing for the look of forgiveness that can be afforded only by the man who resists her. But the cruel punishment that followed her original fault in mocking the Redeemer has destroyed her moral confidence; she has no repertoire of affection, nothing on which to rely in her bid for sympathy, apart from her sexual presence. Her longing for forgiveness is therefore doomed to thwart the search for it. She lives from age to age ever more sunk in sorrow, her desire a kind of rage against men, a misanthropic assault on the sex that cannot assuage her real moral need. She seeks to expiate her fault in acts of service to the knights of the Grail. But the one who serves is not the one who desires and seduces: the split in Kundry's personality can no more be healed than the wound of Amfortas. Only an entirely innocent person (a 'pure fool'), acting from compassion rather than from love or desire, can unite the sundered halves of Kundry's yearning. By resisting her desire he normalizes it, lifts it from the diabolical realm where she otherwise founders, into the light of human dialogue.

In Kundry we witness a sexuality that will always aim to possess and destroy, rather than to cherish the one who gives way to it. It is Wagner's achievement to awaken our sympathy towards this woman who offers sympathy only in her other identity, as the mute and sexless servant of the Grail knights. Her pathetic cry of 'Mitleid mit mir' (compassion for me!) vividly convinces us that, unlike Klingsor, Kundry is not for ever lost, but can be cleansed of the egoism that taints her by the one who understands and forgives her fault.

It is through the character of Kundry, in fact, that we should answer one of the frequently made complaints against Wagner's drama: the complaint that women have been excluded, as though inimical to the search for salvation. Monsalvat is an all-male community and the only woman portrayed in *Parsifal* is both the self-abasing servant of the Order and the demonic agent of its undoing. She is kicked around by the knights and, in her other character, enslaved and humiliated by Klingsor. Not surprisingly, this has given rise to a deep suspicion of the work among feminist writers, some suggesting a hidden sexist agenda, comparable to the hidden anti-Semitic agenda discerned by so many other recent critics.[18] It is perhaps pertinent to make a few remarks in response to this suspicion.

The Wagner operas are all to some extent explorations of the man–woman relation, concerning which neither Wagner nor his contemporaries had views that exactly coincide with those most prevalent today, any more than do Dante's views of the Virgin Mary and her presence in the lives of her devotees. All serious art begins from a core of belief, and the test of a work's value is not the literal truth of that belief, but its truthfulness to what we know and feel of the human heart. To what extent does the work of art bring its world and its life within the orbit of our sympathy, so that we can engage with these things as though they were ours? This is the question entertained by T. S. Eliot in his great essay on 'Poetry and Belief', and it is one that is inevitably in the forefront of the mind when considering the operas of Wagner.[19]

A writer or musician who wishes to glamorize a particular vision of sexual desire and gender roles might attempt to win our sympathy with a puppet version of the man–woman relation, like Lawrence in *Lady Chatterley's Lover*, or with the kind of saccharine picture of feminine devotion associated with the child brides of Dickens. But dramatic objectivity means taking a state of mind, however remote it may be from our own understanding of the world, and building a real and believable character around it. It is thus that Wagner builds the character of Elsa von Brabant around her sexual fantasy of the knight in shining armour – not with words, but with music that is genuinely feminine and loving, and also open to reality and therefore to the seeds of doubt, in this case the doubt that destroys her.

Eva Rieger sees the Wagnerian approach to the man–woman relation as a romanticization of traditional gender roles: the man as decisive, social, law-giving, the woman as private, obedient, full of secrets.[20] This misrepresents Wagner's very real attempt to elevate women into active and often heroic figures. (Consider Brünnhilde, who takes charge of the action through all the tragedies that afflict her, who defies the laws imposed by her father and finally sets fire to the world: a role model if ever there was one.) It also fails to take account of the fact that those traditional gender roles were, at the time, embedded in social reality, and were not aesthetic fictions. To be true to his characters Wagner had to be true to the world in which they were situated. One reason for Wagner's leaning so heavily on myth and legend was that this enabled him to some extent to detach his characters from the burden of day-to-day life in nineteenth-century Germany, so as to open a field of action in which they could realize their full potential, as Brünnhilde does, to alarming effect, at the end of *Götterdämmerung*.

Nietzsche's most interesting criticism was that Wagner did not in fact succeed in creating a believable field of mythic action. To understand Wagner's characters, he advises, we should translate them 'into reality, into the modern – let us be crueller – into the bourgeois!' And what then? We find ourselves among the 'metropolitan' problems of Parisian decadents – 'always five steps from the hospital'.[21]

It is undeniable that the man–woman relation has a central place in Wagner's imagination; but it is impossible to doubt the enormous sympathy for the female sex that permeates his mature dramas. Even the scolding Fricka is given clinching arguments with which to bring her husband down to size, while the abused Sieglinde is, throughout her brief appearance, both heroic and loveable. It is Sieglinde's music – the blessing conferred on Brünnhilde in an extraordinary woman-to-woman moment – that concludes the tetralogy on a note of cosmic tenderness.

There is of course a tendency in Wagner to treat his characters as symbols of universal archetypes – man, woman, the hero, the law-giver and so on. And when characters are eclipsed by the generalities that they stand for, the result is not art but at best allegory, at worst propaganda. But Wagner's characters usually stand proudly above their philosophical baggage, with only occasional lapses – as here and there with Siegfried – when a character might be stuffed into a suitcase and forwarded to his final destination in the realm of ideas.

In *Parsifal* there is one character who carries a weight of philo-sophical baggage beyond the literal actions in which she is involved, and that is Kundry, the *Ewig-weibliche* who is also the bridge between two worlds. But just as it would be a mistake to think of Elsa or Brünnhilde merely as symbols, representing woman in the abstract, so would it be a mistake to think of Kundry as owing her presence in the drama to a piece of romantic philosophy, rather than to the quite definite personality that is given to her by both words and music. Of course, she is not, in the everyday sense, an individual, being the last of many incarnations. But the dramatic context wipes away that fact, and brings her before us as a character with a highly individual voice, awakening feelings that are deep in us all. Only if we understand Kundry in this way, it seems to me, will we grasp the real meaning of *Parsifal*, and the nature of the redemption that is sought throughout the opera and finally granted at the end.

Some commentators have seen Kundry as a symbol of the destruc-tiveness of female sexuality, the trap that lies in wait for the unsuspecting man, and which will enmesh him in a web of demean-ing embraces. But that interpretation, it seems to me, shows only a very superficial grasp of her character, and also of the place of sexual feeling in the world of Monsalvat. Sexual desire stands at the centre of Wagner's dramas because of its semi-divine nature. It is through sexual desire that new relations are embarked on and new human beings conceived: society is at risk in this as in no other peaceful social project, and the taint of abuse and manipulation will survive all attempts to wash it away. Hence ideas of the sacred and the desecrated congregate in our sexuality as nowhere else in human life. *Parsifal*, conceived as an exploration of the sacred, and of the great labour of consecration that is involved in producing and maintaining it, cannot therefore turn away from the moment of sexual desire, or refrain from showing its danger.

For this reason the adverse sexual encounter serves, dramatically, as a symbol of every form of existential pollution – every way in which we can be trapped, cajoled or tempted into relations that we look on with a sense of pollution. Act II of *Parsifal* presents four such contaminating relations: Klingsor's enslavement of Kundry as a sex-object; his voyeuristic desire to corrupt the pure and beautiful Parsifal, whose physical attributes clearly excite Klingsor as he anticipates the sight of Parsifal in Kundry's arms; the trivial promiscuity of the flower-maidens, for whom the object of lust can always be exchanged for a better one; and the intensely targeted soul-lust of Kundry, who seeks to restore what she has lost, to lift herself above her fallen state, and whose devious and cherishing desire for Parsifal has only the self-centred part of compassion.

Wagner's immaculate portrait of these things shows his hero emerging with full knowledge of their subjective power; it also situates them and him in the force-field of religious feeling. It is not just the chivalric story and its basis in celibacy that has this effect. Existential guilt seeks just such a remedy; to restore right relations with the world, to wash away the stain of abuse, guilt and unworthiness, you must change your life. And life is changed by an act of consecration. Act II of *Parsifal* is an illustration of this truth, and Kundry's cry of 'Sehnen . . . Sehnen!' is a call for the existential rescue that will end her suffering by uniting her warring natures in a single and undivided self. It is part of her grandeur that she can play this role, and it is one that no man could easily imitate. Kundry surely stands alongside Medea and Cleopatra as a disturbing female archetype, trapped by circumstance but true to her own demonic nature. She is not just dominated, but also contaminated, by Klingsor's merciless power over her. Everything she does, and everything she feels, even the extremes of her sexual desire, belongs to the attempt to slither free from the control that pollutes her, into a place where love, freedom and purity will at last be hers.

In considering her relation to the man who has enslaved her, it is worth recalling the words of Thomas Mann in his well-known essay on 'The Sorrows and Grandeur of Richard Wagner':

> There is about all Wagner's heroines a touch of grand hysteria, something somnambulistic, enraptured and visionary, which lends a curious and disquieting modernity to their romantic posturings. But the figure of Kundry, 'the rose of hell', is nothing less than an exercise in mythical pathology; in her agonizingly schizoid condition, as instrument of the Devil and penitent hungering after redemption, she is portrayed with an unsparing clinical accuracy, an audacious naturalism in the exploration and representation of a hideously diseased emotional existence, that has always seemed to me a supreme triumph of insight and artistry. Nor is she the only character in *Parsifal* whom Wagner has pushed to the psychological limit. When it says, in the preliminary draft of this last and most extreme work, that Klingsor is the daemon of secret sin, the wild ragings of impotence in the face of sin, we feel ourselves transported into a world of Christian insight into remote and hellish psychological states – the world of Dostoevsky.[22]

Mann is surely right to see Klingsor in those Dostoevskian terms. Klingsor's entire being is an act of defiance – defiance of his own condition, and a negation of the community to which he cannot belong. He is 'outside the communion', excommunicated from the regime of fellowship. And this is shown in his way of dominating Kundry, using his knowledge of her innermost faults in order to bend her to his will and threaten her with the self-image that she abhors. In Klingsor Wagner paints an exemplary portrait of evil, one that is all the more persuasive on account of the dramatic situation. *Parsifal* shows evil as *cast out* from the good, a negation of life's affirmative; as such it must inevitably seek revenge against the community that excludes it.

The question of evil occupied Wagner in all his mature work. Ortrud in *Lohengrin*, Hagen in *Götterdämmerung* and above all Klingsor in *Parsifal* are the fruits of a profound meditation on the mystery of destruction. As Wagner was aware, we distinguish people who are evil from those who are merely bad. Bad people are like you or me, only worse. They belong in the community, even if they behave badly towards it. We can reason with them, improve them, come to terms with them and sometimes accept them. Even if they wreak destruction, like Siegfried, it tends to be because, through deception or manipulation, matters have slipped from their control. But evil people are not like that. They do not belong in the community, even when residing within its territory. Their bad behaviour may be too secret and subversive to be noticeable, and any dialogue with them will be, on their part, a pretence. There is, in them, no scope for improvement, no path to acceptance, and their faults are not of the normal, remediable human variety, but have another and more meta-physical origin. They are visitors from another sphere, incarnations of the Devil. Even their charm – and it is a recognized fact that evil people are often charming – is only further proof of their Otherness. They are, in some sense, the negation of humanity, wholly and unnat-urally at ease with the thing that they seek to destroy. Their presence in the community involves a mingling of elements that do not belong together, and their charm is sorcery: they are, indeed, the most potent form of pollution.

That characterization of evil is summarized in the famous line that Goethe gives to Mephistopheles:

> Ich bin der Geist der stets verneint
> [I am the spirit that for ever negates]

Whereas the bad person is guided by self-interest, to the point of ignor-ing or overriding the others who stand in his path, the evil person is profoundly interested in others, has almost selfless designs on them. His aim is not to use them, as Faust uses Gretchen, but to rob them of themselves. Mephistopheles hopes to steal and destroy Faust's soul and, en route to that end, to destroy the soul of Gretchen. Nowadays we might use the word 'self' instead of 'soul'. But this word is only another name for the same metaphysical mystery around which our lives are built – the mystery of the 'I', which is the centre of conscious-ness and the origin of choice. Evil people are not necessarily threats to the body; but they are threats to the self. They open the deepest spiritual wounds in order to fill them with poison. Such is Klingsor in his abuse of Kundry. His failure to belong to the community does not lead to resignation or despair. It leads to an insightful, almost intimate destruction of the woman whom he tortures, and through whom he also brings destruction to those who have enjoyed the blessedness that he vainly longs for. The world of the evil person is a loveless world, in which intimacy takes the form of domination. To be close to an evil person is to be in his power, since he tolerates no other relationship; hence every intimacy that he achieves merely reinforces his utter loneliness, the metaphysical vacuum of the I that has never said 'thou'. To live without the I/Thou relationship is to lose the benefit of love: it is to relate to others by spells and sorcery, thus by-passing their humanity for the sake of a purely self-centred control.

Encountering evil of the Klingsor kind we sense the existence of a contest between being and nothingness, creation and destruction, and that we are involved in that contest and are saved or jeopardized by our own behaviour. Seen as part of this contest our faults can weigh us down: we seek exoneration, without knowing the human person to whom an appeal for forgiveness can be made. We exist as though suspended above a chasm, ready at any moment to fall. This is what is meant by original sin, and indeed Schopenhauer rewrote the idea of original sin so that it became 'the crime of existence itself' – *die Schuld des Daseins*, the guilt of *existing as an individual*, in free relations with our kind.[23]

Such feelings prompt the great yearning that finds a voice in tragic art and which engages with our most urgent loves and fears in this world: the yearning for the blessing that relieves us of our guilt – guilt that is the inevitable result of our free dealings with others. Glimpses of this blessing are afforded by such liminal experiences as falling in love, recovering from illness, becoming a parent, and encountering in awe the sublime works of nature. At these moments we stand at the threshold of the transcendent, reaching out to what cannot be attained or known. And that to which we reach must be understood in personal terms, since only then does it offer an answer to the unspoken question of our being: the question why? It is the soul of the world, which smiles from the meadows at Monsalvat on Good Friday.

This reaching for that which is both transcendent and personal engages also with the ethic of pollution and taboo. It animates the distinction between the sacred and the profane. And it gives sense to the ideas of good and evil. The supreme blessing, the forgiveness once earned by the Redeemer, is also a purification, a cleansing of the spirit, and an overcoming of alienation. It is this that we glimpse and reach for in prayer and in those moments when our spirit opens to the sublime. In those moments we accept our being as a gift – it has been *bestowed* on us, whether or not by a creator God. And in the encounter with evil we see the opposite of this gift, the negative force that *takes away* what has been given, and which focuses especially on the person, the soul, the place where the given-ness of being can be most clearly revealed and understood, and most spectacularly destroyed.

Those thoughts and experiences represent a kind of deposit in the mind of the moral being – not an explicit theory of the world, but a residue of individual existence, which gathers like the leaf-mould in the forest, feeding the plants that feed it. In the light of those thoughts, good and evil, sacred and profane, redemption, purity and sacrifice all begin to make sense to us, and we are guided along a path of reconciliation, both to the people around us, and to our own destiny as dying things. Such is the religion of Monsalvat, founded in the perpetual memory of the Redeemer, who sanctified our lives through his death, and whose example points the way to a new attempt at redemption. The innocent outsider, perhaps free from specific religious beliefs yet with a heart open to the Redeemer's sacred message, is the one who can bring to this community the only thing that can possibly rescue it, namely the compassion that it has lost.

The Parsifal who stumbles into Monsalvat in Act I sees the world of plants and animals as a field for joyful adventure in which he himself is the thing that matters. Under the influence of Gurnemanz, he learns that animals can suffer, and depend on our help and sympathy. Through Kundry he learns to distinguish pure from polluted love. Finally he learns that, thanks to the sacrifice of Good Friday, nature can smile with the joy of a thing that is cared for. Into this aspect of Parsifal's character Wagner poured all his feelings for animals and his belief in our duty to protect them. At the risk of moralizing he allows Gurnemanz to include tenderness towards the rest of nature as a part of our religious duty, so blending (here as elsewhere) the Christian and the Buddhist conceptions of salvation.

The three tableaus of Wagner's triptych belong together, and display a deep unity – a holistic experience that is the life of religion in its entirety. The three troubled characters – Amfortas, Kundry and Klingsor – belong together, and as the drama proceeds, the relations of dependence that unite them, and which tie each of them to Parsifal's redeeming mission, become ever stronger and tighter. Each is an outcast, a source of pollution. As with Oedipus, the person with wrong relations becomes the wrong kind of thing, one who is on the wrong side of an existential boundary. Klingsor's self-mutilation gave him magic powers with which to defy the human world, to live in domination over others, neither giving nor receiving love, but triumphing in the destruction of those who feel the need for it. His flaw is the extreme one, of standing to the community in a relation of unmitigated malice, with no other goal than destruction. He is the *Geist der stets verneint*, the negation of those whom he encounters, and specifically of Kundry and Amfortas. He is also, as his mutilation indicates, the negation of himself.

Kundry's wrong relations began with the Saviour, whom she mocked in his hour of suffering. Cursed, she lives in torment, needing love and forgiveness but finding only sexual exploitation – hers of others, and others of her. Vampire-like she sucks the blood from others' being, as she sucked the need and guilt from the story of Parsifal's life before regurgitating it in a kiss. Her loneliness is as great as Klingsor's, but she longs to emerge from it in a place of forgiveness, where she is in right relation to others and to the world. She haunts the castle of the Grail, in the hope that her redemption may happen there, but she meets with no real understanding, and cannot find the one who will look into her soul. We do not know how far she is conscious at Monsalvat of the Kundry who is Klingsor's slave, though both women possess the knowledge that has come to Kundry as she wanders between lives and worlds. All we know is that she exists in helpless longing – 'Sehnen . . . Sehnen' – and in a far from helpless need to serve – 'Dienen . . . dienen', the only words she utters in Act III.

Amfortas's weakness led him to fall at the crucial moment into Kundry's arms, and from that has flowed all his woes. Someone who lives by sacred vows lives both in greater certainty that he is rightly related to his fellows, and in greater jeopardy, should he betray them. Amfortas cannot repair his wrong relations to the Grail knights since, by letting the Spear fall into profane hands, he has committed the primal pollution, the desecration of the sanctuary and therefore of the community dedicated to its maintenance. Monsalvat begins to decay, Titurel dies, with more and more knights tempted away by Klingsor's magic and the call of the Spear; soon the pitiless demand that Amfortas fulfil his office turns to outright aggression. Only the return of the Spear can rectify the situation, but Amfortas is powerless to achieve this. He can be helped only by an outsider, a stranger to the community who is foolish enough to enter the castle of Klingsor, and pure enough to resist what he finds there.

These three characters are bound in mutual dependence by the very characteristics that forbid any fruitful relation – Kundry as Klingsor's slave and Amfortas's seducer; Amfortas as the invalid whom Kundry serves; Klingsor as Kundry's master and the envious rival of Amfortas, and so on. In every sense they are worlds apart; but they are bound together in a tight knot of anguish, symbolized by the internal connection between the motifs that evoke them. They illustrate the many forms of wrong relations, and the places from which the cry of anguish comes. Parsifal enters their linked worlds without any relations at all. He has never known his father, has abandoned his mother, and has no resource in these novel situations save the emotion that distinguishes him – *Mitleid*, the ability not just to feel from within what another suffers, but to take the other's burden on himself. Yet this, we discover, is exactly what is needed, not only to reunite the sundered halves of Kundry, but also to remain true in the moment of temptation, so as to return to Amfortas with the Spear. As for Klingsor he must vanish, along with his realm of magic, since the negative that he had directed at others is now turned solely on himself.

Wagner saw, and saw more deeply than any artist of his time, that the religious way of life is neither a passing moment in history nor dependent on some given culture. Religion lies deep in human nature, and the appeal for redemption, while answered with exemplary courage by Christ, comes from mankind as a whole. The cry – 'Sehnen . . . Sehnen' – is answered by the Buddha too, and in every form it has no other answer than *Mitleid*, in the broadest sense of putting others and their suffering before myself and my desires. For this to be a real answer to the cry of longing, and to the woe that is our inevitable inheritance, we need right relations with our kind, from which guilt and contamination have been cleansed. And we reach for the ritual that expresses this fact, which reconciles us to our fellows and to ourselves, and shows us that we face death together and as a part of the eternal renewal of our shared and mysterious world.

There is a kind of deep acceptance of the human condition laid before us by the music of *Parsifal*, and it is against the background of this acceptance that the tasks of redemption and consecration are defined. Suffering and relief, guilt and forgiveness, fragmentation and restoration, are intrinsically connected in the drama, calling to each other through the score. It is our woe that summons the Redeemer, and our sin that calls for the sacrifice. This sense of unity is itself a symbol of the religious worldview, an icon of the inner connectedness that changes reality from something random, contingent and meaningless to a self-sustaining and radiant whole – a change, as the Hindus express it, from samsara to Brahman. The musical material fragments and re-forms in response to the diverse emotions, and then brings them together in an all-comprehending resolution that has been earned dramatically and musically. We are being led through a musico-poetic argument that shows woe and redemption, guilt and forgiveness, to be mutually dependent aspects of a life fully lived. Whatever doubts we may have about the characters and the drama, there is, in the music itself, a process of healing and making whole that is emblematic of the dedicated way of life. Like the primordial religious ritual, the music invites us to come home to what we are.

4

Sin, Love and Redemption

Christianity is acknowledged in *Parsifal*, but only as one strand in a web of predicaments, many of which challenge the Christian world-view. References to eternal life are vague suggestions in the ritual, which is the central *fact* of the Monsalvat religion, and the ritual itself is an artful adaptation of the Christian Eucharist to a community that looks on the sacred moment not as a foreshadowing of the afterlife but as a shining in the here and now. Titurel's hope is not for eternal life, but for the extra spell of life granted by the sight of the Grail, and in the context of the drama this is a highly destructive hope – destructive most of all of Titurel's son, who is mercilessly subjected to the greatest agony in order that his father should cling for a little longer to his pointless tenancy. All this suggests that Christianity is being questioned rather than affirmed in the wider narrative.

In this connection we must recognize the symbolic importance of Titurel. The ghostly father lingers thus in all of us, barking out orders and sharpening our guilt. As 'our Father, which art in Heaven', he is the divine law-giver and object of religious submission. He is the 'I', the centre of decision, that speaks through the Old Testament and the Koran, the 'I am that I am' who addressed Moses from the burning bush, refusing to name himself except as the all-observing first-person singular. His voice is still heard in the rites of the Christian religion, though not in the communion displayed in *Parsifal*. In *Parsifal* he has been dethroned, reduced to a ghostly remainder, object of duty and contrition, borrowing his meagre life from our sin. The community of the Grail will be revived when he is finally buried.

Such is the father, as he appears in *Parsifal*: a stunning anticipation of the shadow that haunts Kafka's stories, a looming absence reminding Amfortas at every moment of his failure and his guilt. There is also a mother who, being dead, can present no rival 'I' that might soften the father's bleak imperatives. Herzeleide died from her son but does not condemn him; Titurel lives from his son, but condemns him to suffer. Both speak from the tomb, the one through her proxy, Kundry, the other in person. Herzeleide speaks of love, and the sorrow of love, Titurel of law and obedience. Herzeleide speaks to Parsifal not with the 'I' of command, but with the 'thou' of tenderness and sorrow. She too is an object of guilt, but her message is one of love and compassion, not law. This message prepares her son for his redeeming task, which is to rescue the other son, Amfortas, from the guilt and pain that are destroying him. The transition from law to love will then be complete, and the stern rule of the Father replaced by mutual sympathy, which is the religion of the Son.

In that way we can see the action of *Parsifal* as an allegory of the Gospel story, and of the humanizing message of Jesus who, in presenting the cup at the Last Supper, said: 'this is my blood, of the New Covenant'. Those words announce a new religion, and Wagner is taking them literally: the new religion is focused on life, and on blood as the symbol of life; its essence is sacrifice, the blood sacrifice of Christ himself; and its aim is not obedience to the dead hand of the law, but commemoration of the guiltless sacrificial victim, in a 'feast of love'. As noted earlier, Wagner did not believe in God, but in 'godliness, which is revealed in a Jesus *without sin*'.[1] By 'godliness' I understand the attempt to live a pure life within sacred boundaries, not exerting power over others but approaching them in a spirit of sympathy. On this understanding, as Wagner rightly insists, a person can be godly without the belief in God. And if he does believe in God, it is not the creator or the loving guide, but God the sufferer, the new God of Christianity, who dies for the sake of human beings. Thus we find Wagner writing to King Ludwig in 1865, with the following words:

Today it is once more Good Friday. Oh Holy Day! Most significant for the world! Day of Redemption. God in suffering. Who can take the tremendous scale of it? And yet, even as it lies beyond words, so it is the closest thing of all to mankind. God the Creator, he must lie entirely beyond the grasp of the world; God the loving guide, he can be inwardly loved, but not understood; but God the sufferer, he writes himself inwardly in our hearts; this tremendous anguish washes away the stubbornness of life. God is in us; the world is vanquished. Who created it? Useless question. Who overcame it? God in our hearts – the God that is grasped in the deepest pain of fellow feeling.[2]

Although that captures a deep truth in Christianity, we should not see the promise of eternity as an accidental addition to the Christian religion. Take that promise away and what remains is religion of a very different kind – one in which the vital distinctions that inform Wagner's drama, between the sacred and the profane, the pure and the polluted, the fallen and the saved, require some other foundation than the Christian theology of hope.[3] At the same time, *Parsifal* is suggesting, we cannot easily dispense with those distinctions. Through them we understand the purity and commitment that inform right relations with others and with ourselves. Parsifal's mission is not to bring hope for eternal life, but to restore the sanctity of the desecrated relics, and to rebuild a community in which forgiveness prevails over blame. The religious life of the restored Monsalvat is not one devoted to another life beyond the grave; for that would be merely an extension of *chronos* time, of the kind craved by Titurel. The new religious life transforms *chronos* to *kairos*: it invites us to stand back from desire and dominion, so as to look on life as it is, from a stance of commiserating sympathy.

Hence the religion of *Parsifal* is built from sacraments, but sacraments that have been cleansed of all reference to the transcendental. The sacred, Wagner believed, is a deep and inextinguishable human need, and all his mature music dramas explore some aspect of it. According to the Latin etymology a sacrifice (*sacrificium*, from *sacrum facere*) is something *made* sacred. And we answer to the need for the sacred through sacrifices of the kind put before us by the Redeemer. The action of *Parsifal* involves a meditation on this process.

Sacrifices are of two kinds: things offered and things suffered. We offer sacrifices *to* our gods; we also make sacrifices *for* them.[4] Many ancient religions focus on sacrificial victims, killed on the altar in propitiation of a god. The sacrificial offering is a gift to the god from the worshippers, and forms the central episode in the rite. In the

Christian religion, however, things are reversed. The sacrificial offering is a gift from the god to the worshippers, who receive the body and blood of the divine victim, remembering his suffering when he gave himself to the world.

The transition from the pagan and Hebrew to the Christian view of sacrifice is at the forefront of Wagner's thinking in *Parsifal*, as is the double meaning of sacrifice, as something both offered and suffered. Theological doctrines may strive to make sense of this; but it is not the doctrines that matter so much as the extraordinary melding of emotions, the quasi-dramatic unity achieved by the communion ceremony, in which suffering, contrition, forgiveness and love are somehow distilled together to become an exaltation of the spirit and a taste in the mouth.

The ritual is not a representation of Christ's Passion, but a re-enactment of it. In the Roman Catholic liturgy the bread and the wine are supposedly transubstantiated into Christ's body and blood, so that the dying God becomes a 'real presence' at the altar. By this ritual (the 'communion') the worshippers, if they have confessed their sins and done proper penance, are purified, renewing their place among the 'saved'. Rituals must be repeated exactly otherwise they lose their power – which is a power to incorporate, to cleanse, to repossess each member in the community's name. Hence the Eucharist must be celebrated again and again, if the community is to be maintained in a state of redemption, and it cannot be shortened, adjusted or varied for the benefit of anyone involved in it, least of all for the benefit of the one who conducts the ceremony, and who mediates between the assembled individuals and the kingdom of salvation. This we know from the history of the Eucharist, in which whole communities have been condemned, banished or even massacred, like the Old Believers in Russia, for some unsanctified amendment to the words, the images or the gestures displayed at the altar.

In *Parsifal* there is just such an amendment to the Eucharistic words: the blood is turned to wine, not wine to blood. For the Grail was held to Christ's wounds, and contains his blood, from which the abundance of goods, of which wine is a fitting symbol, flows to his devotees. In Monsalvat the communion ceremony exists in a specific local version, which already speaks of the isolation of the knights from the world beyond the boundary of nowhere. But it retains the crucial element that fascinated Wagner and which is a theme throughout the action of *Parsifal*: the element of consecration. Consecration is something that we human beings do, and the sanctity that results from it is received, in our feelings, as a transformation, a *Verwandlung*, into another state of being. Such is expressed in the music of Wagner's communion.

Many writers have commented on the close resemblance between the Eucharistic drama and the mystery cults of antiquity, and on the reminiscence of Greek tragedy, itself part of the ancient festival of Dionysus. Anthropologists associate the Lamb of God who is sacrificed on mankind's behalf with the scapegoat of Leviticus, who carries the sins of the community into the wilderness, there to purge them through a miserable death. Influenced by Sir James Frazer and the armchair anthropologists,[5] by Mircea Eliade and Jessie Weston, we are likely to see the Eucharist in terms of such a general theory of the sacrificial offering, who becomes sacred in the moment of sacrifice, and whose flesh must be broken and consumed, in order that the world should be renewed.

One such general theory – and one of the most influential – is that of René Girard, who has argued that the sense of the sacred originates in violence, and that the paradigm form of religious violence is the collective murder of a victim.[6] In the absence of a judicial system, Girard argues, societies are invaded by 'mimetic desire', as rivals struggle to match each other's social and material acquisitions, so heightening antagonism and precipitating the cycle of revenge. The solution is to identify a victim, one marked by fate as 'outside' the community and therefore not entitled to vengeance against it, who can be the target of the accumulated blood-lust, and who can bring the chain of retribution to an end. Scapegoating is society's way of re-creating 'difference' and so restoring itself. By uniting against the scapegoat people are released from their rivalries and reconciled.

Girard adds a corollary to his anthropological observations, and one that is surely influenced by Wagner. Jesus, Girard argues, was the first sacrificial victim who *clearly understood* what was being done to him, and in exchange for the suffering inflicted by his tormentors offered them the equivalent in forgiveness. This extraordinary reversal of the sacrificial logic did not merely set an example to Christ's followers. It showed us how to renounce the demands of the will so as to look with compassion on all that suffers. Thereafter violence was no longer needed, and rivalry would be the signal for reconciliation and forgiveness rather than sacrificial murder. Christ's sacrifice, so understood, was the *last* sacrifice, the sacrifice that brought the hunger for victims to an end.

Although Wagner's treatment of the Gospel story corresponds in some ways to Girard's, it attempts to lay the foundation for a more rational theology of forgiveness. On Girard's view we overcome our rivalries, hatreds and jealousies by offloading them on to the scapegoat, who then dies from the burden. He has 'taken away the sins of the world', and we love him accordingly, since he enables us to begin the difficult task of reconciliation with each other.[7] Wagner's vision, as expressed in *Parsifal* and in the unfinished drama of *Jesus of Nazareth*, sketched in 1848–9, emphasizes the compassion of the Redeemer, who teaches another way of being and another form of knowledge. There is a sense in which Christ paid the price of our sins, showing us that *this* is what we deserve. But his sacrifice does not take away the sins of the world. Rather it sets an example, from which we learn the paltriness of our selfish appetites. The redemptive quality of sacrifice does not consist in conveying us to another world where we live in bliss for ever, but in transforming our vision of *this* world. Through compassion the Redeemer made a gift of himself, and we, by following that example, learn to do the same, to make of what we are and do a gift to others, rather than a claim for ourselves. Then, bound in a new relation of love, we renew the world, which flowers like the meadows on Good Friday.

That vision of sacrifice restores the element that we witness so clearly in the old Hebrew stories of Cain and Abel, and Abraham and Isaac, and which plays only a subordinate role in Girard's theory, namely the element of gift. Violence is not the origin or essence of sacrifice, but the result of it. It comes about when the thing that must be given is a life, and a life can be given only when a living creature is killed. Abraham accepts that he must surrender Isaac when God commands him to do so, since Isaac was a gift from God. The unusual feature of Christ's sacrifice was that this supreme gift – the offering up of a life – was not from man to God but from God to man. And that raises the question of what man must give in return. Christians believe that they can offer no real equivalent of the supreme gift that they have received: all they can do is to live in a more godly way, in humility, repentance and neighbour-love. The mass and the service of Holy Communion are centred on that idea. According to Christian doctrine, however, Christ, in dying for our sins, offered more than forgiveness: he offered life everlasting, and underscored the offer with his own Resurrection.

In the communion of the Grail knights the emphasis is not on confession, repentance and forgiveness, but on the nourishment provided by the Redeemer's flesh and blood. It is the death of the Redeemer, not his Resurrection, that is the salvation of the world, for it is in his death that he gave himself as a sacrificial offering. Indeed, the Resurrection is nowhere mentioned. Hence the renewal celebrated at Easter occurs, in Monsalvat, on Good Friday, and not on Easter Sunday. The renewal of the world lies in the Eucharist itself, the ritual through which we re-enact the death of the Redeemer, and take him into ourselves. In some way the world was changed by the Redeemer's sacrifice, and everything thereafter has stood in the light of his gift. We constantly stray from the path of holiness, but through the memory of the Redeemer's sacrifice, re-enacted in the Eucharist, we re-consecrate our lives.

However, we might wonder what the work of consecration really achieves. The world portrayed in *Parsifal* is a harsh, even pitiless world. In punishment for her mockery of the Redeemer, Kundry is driven from life to life, hungry for the love and forgiveness that are always withheld from her. In punishment for his one grave transgression, in losing the Spear while entwined in Kundry's arms, Amfortas must endure endless agony from a wound that does not heal. He longs to die on the altar before which he bleeds. But no such mercy is offered him. His heart-rending appeals to the *All-Erbarmer* are met by silence, and we gradually understand that there is no divine power that could rectify Amfortas's suffering, which is renewed by the very act through which the Redeemer is remembered.

The Redeemer visited this world once and only once. Nothing is left of him save the trace entrusted to the knights of the Grail: the vessel containing his blood and the Spear that pierced his side. There is no second coming, and no God to perpetuate the compassion that the Redeemer poured out on us. The music confirms this picture: again and again it takes contrition to the limit, raising imploring hands, as in the transformation scenes, to a Heaven that takes no notice of the gesture. If there is such a thing as redemption in this bleak and forsaken world, then it is only a human being who could offer it. Salvation must come from our own resources, and the Redeemer is a 'real presence' among us only fictively, in the act of communion in which nothing is more striking than the fact that the Redeemer isn't there.

For Wagner, as for Girard, the sacred and the sacrificial are at root the same idea. But Wagner sees the sacrifice of Christ as part of the wider posture of consecration. In *Parsifal*, things, people and rituals are sacred because we have made them so, by an act that purifies them of sin and pollution and restores the right relations with others on which our salvation depends. This 'making sacred' of our earthly life is, I argued in the second chapter, conveyed in the music, and above all in the music of the communion. But it is also directly portrayed in Act III, in the scene in which Kundry washes the feet of Parsifal, Gurnemanz anoints Parsifal as king, and Parsifal baptizes Kundry. It is one of those moments in the opera, suspended between embarrassing excess and didactic clarity, when spectators might be as easily repulsed as moved by what they see. The image of the penitent Magdalene, so blatantly summoned like a page from a kitsch religious calendar, wars with the sublime inwardness of the consecration motif (44). No matter, perhaps, given that the Good Friday music is about to flood the scene, conveying the effect of consecration as no theology could hope to rival. Nevertheless the artistic intention here is as bold as could be, asking us to believe that an act of purification has occurred, which will enable Parsifal to perform the sacred office of the Eucharist and the no-longer-heathen Kundry to participate, so as to shuffle off her many mortal coils.

Although referred to again and again by the protagonists, the Redeemer enters the story only as someone *thought about*, and thought about in one connection, namely his death as a sacrificial offering. Sometimes, as in Gurnemanz's Good Friday sermon, this death is described as an atonement for the sins of the world. But it is not an atonement that has purchased eternal life for the rest of us, nor has it contributed in any observable way to the relief of the suffering on stage. Without the Crucifixion there would have been no Grail, no Spear, no bequest of the holy relics, and therefore no wound in the side of Amfortas; and without the Crucifixion there would have been no occasion for Kundry's mockery and for the terrible punishment through which she has been forced to pay for it. All that the Redeemer has conferred on Monsalvat is his death and the ritual by which it is remembered. What good has he done, therefore, and why was his sacrifice required?

Among the answers suggested in the drama and the music of *Parsifal*, two in particular gain purchase as the plot unfolds, namely: discipleship and acceptance. By following the Redeemer's example we exchange power for love and resentment for forgiveness, in all the ways that life might offer us. The Redeemer's gift was to show that this is possible. Suffering lies in the nature of things. There is no God who has ordained it, and no God who can extinguish it. Forgiveness and compassion are our sole resources, and discipleship means extending them as the Redeemer might have extended them, to the ones into whose presence we are called. Such is the love that was offered to mankind on the cross – the love that we receive by loving others in turn.

However, the path of discipleship is precarious. We wander away from it in ways that jeopardize the very gift that the Redeemer brought to us. Thus when one of the relics was lost and the king wounded, the communion of the Grail fell immediately into disorder. The knights turned on their ruined king with a pitiless savagery that far exceeded his deserts. The Redeemer would surely not have countenanced such cruelty, even if the gift of his blood was in part the cause of it. Discipleship, as presented in *Parsifal*, is an ambivalent undertaking, as likely to lead to sadistic abuse as to the love displayed by the Redeemer.

The second answer to our question seems more promising. Throughout the opera the orchestra is uniting, dividing and uniting again the constants of the human condition: suffering and compassion, sin and forgiveness, desolation and blessedness are intermingled, each embracing the terms laid down by the other. The cries of woe ring out in the transformation scene of Act I above the eternally recurring circle of fifths, telling us that things were ever thus and will be thus for ever. The themes of pain and contrition are woven into the *Grundthema*, which raises its hands to Heaven before sinking through the gamut of our troubles back to earth. The resolute up-beat of the Spear motif, which pushes the pure fool onward in his search for home, reaches no triumphant conclusion but only a dying fall, a 'sorrowful look of love' that shines through the elaborate cadence before dwindling to nothing. And so it must be: for without suffering there can be no compassion, without sin no forgiveness, and without desolation no restoration and no joy. And

> It is right it should be so
> Man was made for Joy and Woe
> And when this we rightly know
> Thro the World we safely go
> Joy and Woe are woven fine
> *A Clothing for the soul divine* . . .

The sense of wholeness that Blake invokes in his 'Auguries of Inno-cence' is present throughout Parsifal, in a score that gathers from the stage all the painful fragments of the human condition, all our long-ings and transgressions, and returns them at the last healed and unified, in a radiant icon of acceptance. And included in this accept-ance is the pitiless ritual of Monsalvat, which the innocent outsider has been called to rectify.

This brings me to the crucial idea on which the action of Parsifal turns: the idea of *Mitleid*, or compassion. In English usage 'pity' (which is etymologically connected to 'piety') has different con-notations from Latin 'compassion', Greek 'sympathy' and German *Mitleid*, all equivalent to 'suffering with'. (Italian *pietà* means both pity and piety.) In reaction to Nietzsche's vehement critique of pity as the negation of life and the 'practice of nihilism'[8] it is common to distinguish pity from compassion, the first supposedly fixated on suffering, the second striving to remedy it. On the other hand what Nietzsche attacked was *Mitleid*, the exact German translation of 'compassion' and 'sympathy'. 'Mitleid' means 'suffering with', and it is both the 'suffering' and the 'with' that Nietzsche objected to. Through *Mitleid*, he argued, we weaken ourselves, and also join ourselves to what is inferior to us. In whatever way we may strive to moderate Nietzsche's critique, there is no doubt that he would have applied it to the pure fool, *durch Mitleid wissend*, of Wagner's drama.

The distinction between *Mitleid* as pity, condemned by Nietzsche, and *Mitleid* as compassion, advocated by Schopenhauer, is a fertile theme of philosophy.[9] And it is a distinction marked out by ordinary ways of talking. Often we say 'I pity you' by way of expressing our anger and contempt, and in all uses the term 'pity' expresses an unequal relation, in which the pitying party stands above the one whom he pities. For this reason we cannot easily love someone whom we pity, since love is a relation of equality, a giving that hopes for a gift in return. Moreover the object of pity will, if he retains his self-respect, shrink from those who look down on him. The term 'compassion' has no such negative connotations.

We should also distinguish both pity and compassion from sympathy, which is an attitude that is both good in itself, and a blessing bestowed on others. Unlike compassion sympathy extends as much to the good things that happen to us as to the bad. Thus we can sympathize with another's joy and good humour, as well as with his pain.

Clearly there are many vital distinctions here, and Wagner's drama is leading us into overgrown moral territory. Nietzsche thinks of pity as a weakness to be overcome. Compassion, as displayed in *Parsifal*, is not a weakness but a strength. But Parsifal's compassion is not the attitude that is so frequently praised in Schopenhauer's writings. For Schopenhauer compassion is a way of negating the will, and so rescuing ourselves from the compulsion to cling to our life as individuals. If Wagner's central character is really in the business of turning away from life, rather than offering a better form of it, then why does he go to so much trouble on behalf of Amfortas, and on behalf of Kundry too, in his long and painful journey of redemption? Parsifal's compassion, which leads him to take on burden after burden, and to venture into the world of sin and despair, is clearly a way of engaging with life rather than a way of avoiding it, and engaging at the deepest level.

Interestingly the first edition of the poem of *Parsifal*, issued before it had been set to music, ends not with the evocation of the Redeemer, but with the lines:

> Gross ist der Zauber der Begehrens
> Grösser ist der Kraft des Entsagens.

(Great is the magic of desire, greater is the strength of renunciation.) This Schopenhauerean sentiment is there in all the other late operas; but *Parsifal*, in its final realization, takes a stand against it. Redemption, in *Parsifal*, is not renunciation, but compassion, and compassion means an active confrontation with suffering, on behalf of someone else.

One thing is immediately clear, moreover, which is that Parsifal's compassion is not just a feeling: it is also a form of knowledge. What kind of knowledge is this? Philosophers distinguish theoretical from practical knowledge – knowledge *that* from knowledge *how*. But that neat distinction does not capture the many subtleties. For example, there is knowledge what to think, knowledge what to do and what to feel. 'Knowledge what' denotes a state of the whole being, and it is acquired through virtue, while 'knowledge how' is acquired through skill. There is such a thing as feeling in ignorance, not responding appropriately to a situation that demands feeling if it is to be properly understood. Our feelings are *about* the world, and therefore stand in judgement upon it. Hence they can be appropriate or inappropriate, right or wrong. Here Wagner stands side by side with those phenomenologists who have argued that it is the intentionality of our emotions that defines the nature of their objects, not the objects, neutrally described, that provide the foundation for what we feel.[10] Such is the knowledge enshrined in the phrase *durch Mitleid wissend*. Not to have this kind of knowledge is to lack a vital input into practical reasoning: it is to be vulnerable to mistakes that cannot be corrected by factual information, or by elementary skills. In ordinary life we sometimes refer to 'emotional knowledge' and 'emotional intelligence', and it is certainly right to speak of emotional education, meaning the acquisition of the virtues that enable us to 'know what to feel' in situations that might otherwise overwhelm us, as Parsifal was overwhelmed by the sight of Amfortas's pain.[11]

When Parsifal shoots the swan it does not occur to him to see his action from any point of view but his own. Through Gurnemanz he sees what he has done from another's point of view, and also from the point of view of the swan. He responds immediately with a remorse that does him credit, even if it is also over the top. He responds to the news of his mother's death with another burst of emotion, equally creditable but equally over the top. When it comes to witnessing the agony of Amfortas so over the top is his response that he is reduced to helpless silence, persuading Gurnemanz that the boy is learning nothing and is therefore not the pure fool who knows through *Mitleid*.

In the second act, however, we see the nature and extent of Parsifal's subsequent discoveries. He is a boy, entering the world with childish laughter. But he has learned to respond to others as they are in themselves, sensing the deep motives within their present feelings, and how those feelings came to be. Kundry's seduction brings her tormented soul into the orbit of his own; he senses her ability both to present and extract confession, to wind another into her love-charms, and thereby to wound him in his very being. This is what Parsifal had inarticulately felt when clutching his heart at the sight of Amfortas. It comes to him now with a clear perception that none other has had except Kundry, who once knew Amfortas's weakness and knew it for what it is. Kundry the seductress has only the half of sympathy – the insight into Amfortas's soul, but not the desire to protect it. In Klingsor's domain Kundry uses her insight against Amfortas, just as Klingsor uses his sadistic insight against Kundry. The other half of sympathy comes to her only when haunting Monsalvat, the remnant and shell of the woman who had caused its ruin.

What we witness in the encounter between Parsifal and Kundry in Klingsor's castle is *Mitleid* in its full meaning: not just 'suffering with' but knowledge; and not knowledge of facts, skills or competences, but an inwardness with another conscious being – a knowledge of 'what it is like' to be Kundry, and 'what it is like' to be the victim of her charms. Amfortas's wound is already implied in his surrender, and Parsifal, he too on the verge of surrender, has a premonition of the wound that inevitably follows, a wound not of the flesh only but of the entire being. The wound is already there in Kundry, and

Parsifal's insight, after he has thrust her away, is that she needs his compassion, and that this compassion will bring her back from the realm of perdition. He has sensed the full story of her sorrow, without explicitly knowing this woman as the Kundry who haunts Monsalvat, seeking there only to serve. The knowledge that comes through compassion is seldom *conscious* knowledge, which is one reason why *Mitleid* is needed: it acquaints us with the emotional landscape of which consciousness knows only a small and over-cultivated patch.

Sometimes the distinction is made between sympathy and empathy – *Mitgefühl* and *Einfühlung, feeling* with another, and *identifying* with another. In an important study St Edith Stein explored some of the distinctions here, and proposed *Einfühlung*, empathy, as one part of the epistemological competence of the rational being.[12] We know other minds, she suggested, by adopting them as our own, and feeling from within the motives and responses through which they represent the world. Whatever the truth in that suggestion, we should not be misled into thinking that empathy is all that Parsifal acquires through his moral apprenticeship. The torturer too has empathy, for it is by knowing from within what his victim is suffering that he fuels his sadistic pleasure. Klingsor is an expert in empathy, as the scene between him and Kundry shows: she cannot flee from his psychological grip, since he knows beforehand exactly which part of her psyche, her memory, her hopes and desires can be pressed upon so as to produce the most exquisite pain. But he has no compassion for her, is devoid of compassion for all other beings, since compassion stands in the way of domination: it is the negation of the lust for power.

Parsifal's purity in one sense shields him from others: he cannot understand them as Klingsor understands Kundry, knowing how to make use of her for goals of his own. In another sense, however, Parsifal is brought closer to others by his purity: for he has only one way of knowing them, which is by crossing the barrier into their inner selfhood, so as to feel what they feel, from the perspective that is theirs. He knows from within what Amfortas is suffering – not physical pain only, but also the emotional turmoil and conflict that comes from a contaminated love. And this empathetic reaction gives rise, in him, to the desire to rescue the other, to bring the other back from destruction. Empathy does not deliver that desire; only sympathy can deliver it; only the sense that the other matters, and that something is at stake in all this suffering, something that must be rectified. The ethic of pollution and taboo is rooted in this sense of an existential defect, of being cast out, and in the world of *Parsifal* such apartness from the world of right relations is what is meant by 'sin'. Repentance, contrition and forgiveness are the process whereby sin is rectified, so that purity comes in the place of pollution: such is the burden of Gurnemanz's Good Friday homily, and the nature of this purity is made sublimely present in the music of that episode.

There is, Parsifal learns, such a thing as restoration and renewal, which comes from the supreme sacrifice that once was made on our behalf, a restoration and renewal that can be obtained by all of us if, like Parsifal, we take up our cross, which means answering the call to rescue another being from suffering and despair. In the vision expressed in *Parsifal*, this rescue of the other is the entirety of religion.

One way of understanding the 'immanent' religion of *Parsifal* is through Kant's critical philosophy, which had a profound influence on Wagner's generation, and which has had an equally profound influence on me. According to the Kantian picture we respond to human beings both as natural objects, governed by causal laws, and as free subjects, accountable for what they do. Those two attitudes are incommensurable.[13] There is no way to squeeze freedom into the web of causal relations, nor can we dismiss freedom as a mere 'appearance' that has no part in the ultimate reality. Human beings are persons for us, and persons are free in that they hold each other to account, asking 'Why?' of all that they are and do. Hence there has emerged a network of concepts, judgements and emotions founded in our mutual recognition as subjects, related to each other as 'I' and 'thou'. When I approach you as a 'thou' I encounter a piece of the natural world that is transfigured by my way of addressing it, the 'I' shining through the material body from that horizon where only you can stand. Seeing you in this way I open myself to your subjective being. I engage with you as an embodied self, a visitor in this world who has also made a home in it.

It is in some such way that we should envisage sacred objects and events. Sacred things intrude into the flow of causality in something like the way subjective freedom intrudes into the realm of natural objects. In the encounter with sacred things we address the 'real presence' of spiritual beings, in events and processes that, seen in another way, are normal parts of the material world. That is how the knights of Monsalvat should understand their communion. In the bread and wine of communion they are to meet the 'I' of Christ.

To a certain measure such moments of consecration give substance to the Monsalvat religion. But it might reasonably be asked what lasting difference they make to the lives and feelings of those who experience them. In traditional Christian religion sacraments are certainly *kairos* moments. But their importance is supposed to lie also in their transformative power – bringing sinners nearer to God, and changing their prospects in the life to come. Does the sacrament in Monsalvat achieve anything at all, apart from the immense suffering of Amfortas as he struggles to perform it?

Wagner was baptized in the Lutheran Church and, at the time that he composed *Parsifal*, was decidedly hostile to the Catholic Church, frequently commenting adversely on it to Cosima. This posture is reflected in a Lutheran view of the Christian sacraments, as these are shown in Acts I and III of the drama. The Roman Catholic Church recognizes seven sacraments, including holy orders, marriage and the anointing of the sick. Calvin reduced the sacraments to two – baptism and communion, the only two that occur in the life of Christ. Luther included penance along with baptism and communion, as the three ways in which we are incorporated into the community of the faithful. Marriage and holy orders are conspicuously absent from the Calvinist and Lutheran list of sacraments, as they are effectively absent from Monsalvat. But baptism and communion occur, and the penance of Amfortas dominates the outer acts.

Those three sacraments have to bear the entire weight of the community's religious need. Although the Grail king has a holy office in presenting the sacrament, he is not in any other sense a priest in holy orders, responsible for the spiritual life of his flock. His community has no settled expectation of living, marrying, reproducing and dying in the arms of a Church. The only baptism we are shown is that of a

heathen, and, although there are children at Monsalvat, they are novices in the sacred order, distant members of the chorus: *ces voix
d'enfants, chantant dans la coupole*.[14] Who knows how they first
arrived there? Doctrine and hope play no real part in the knights'
salvation and immersion in sacred moments is all that the brotherhood offers to those whom it includes. Can that be enough? Can we
have a religion that is purely sacramental, and which offers neither a
Church, nor an afterlife, nor even – it seems – the belief in God the
father, creator of the world?

Those questions point us to the secretive nature of the Eucharist
displayed in *Parsifal*. Detached from the enfolding life of a Church
the ceremony has an enigmatic quality. Although Wagner gives sense
to it through the words of the knights and squires, it is in a certain
measure a secular sense. The blood and body of the Redeemer become
the courage and strength of the knights; they are the food of earthly
deeds and temporal fellowship. The communicants take nothing of
Heaven, and eat what is offered in the same spirit as those who feast
from the Grail in Wolfram's Munsalvaesche. All this is expressed in
the manly marching theme of the love-feast (28).

What has the Redeemer to do with this religion without the afterlife, without the Church, and without God? That is surely among the
most important of all the many questions raised by Wagner's drama.
The Redeemer so often mentioned by the characters is clearly the
Christ of the Gospels, construed not as an incarnate Divinity but as
an exemplary human being. He came among us, not with messages
from on high, but as the thing that he was and is. Indeed, in an
important sense, he *was* the message. His meaning for us, as for the
knights of the Grail, is not transcendental but existential.[15] It is in this
way, I believe, that we must approach the residual Christianity of
Parsifal – the elements of the Gospel message that remain, when all
theological commitments have been subtracted from it.

The sacred ritual represents the great gift of himself that the
Redeemer made. It rehearses the fact that pain and death are not the
meaningless negatives that are apparent to the objective and scientific
eye, but things that might be offered as well as suffered, and offered
as gifts. The thought of this should inspire gratitude, and also a
desire to match the Redeemer's gift with gifts of our own. In the

communion we should come to see the ordinary world of accident, sorrow and suffering in another way, as bound in moral relations, just as we see the smile that shines in another's eyes as a gift and an invitation. As Gurnemanz says to Parsifal, when the latter cries out against the day of the Redeemer's agony 'You see that it is not so.' And we hear that it is not so too. As always Wagner's music rises to the challenge of this sublime moment, and paints in impeccable accents the beauty of the world, when understood as the place of atonement. As in the music of the communion in Act I the world of the Good Friday meadows is consecrated by the music. We hear subjectively what is objectively inaudible, namely the 'given-ness' of our being, and the peace that stems from recognizing this – the 'peace which passeth all understanding' (Phillipians 4:7).

That is how Gurnemanz understands the sacred order in which he participates. But it is clear that the knights have lost sight of what Good Friday really means. It is Parsifal's mission to restore what they have lost.

He does not stumble into Monsalvat in order to preach doctrines or to lay down laws. He is there to be himself, and to show through his example what the life of compassion really requires of us. He gives an existential proof of his own purity – showing to those nearest to him, who are a collection of oddballs and misfits in many ways comparable to those who adhered to Christ, that *they exist fully* for him, that he suffers *with* them, and that for this very reason they are healed, which is to say, incorporated into the community whose bond of love he has come to restore.

Parsifal's purity is a posture towards the other, a willingness to relate to the other openly, honestly and without manipulation. This is what Parsifal showed to Kundry in their shared *kairos* moment, and which planted in her the seed of her own salvation. The tension between purity, so conceived, and the corruptions that threaten it can be expressed in Schopenhauerian or in Buddhist terms, as well as in the terms of the Gospel narrative. For Schopenhauer it is a tension between the renunciation of will through the knowledge granted by compassion and existence subordinate to will. For the Buddhist it is the tension between *anatta*, the denial of self, which is the first stage to liberation from the cycle of being, and *samsara*, life in this world.

For the Buddhist the path to salvation involves the recognition of suffering (*dukkha*), and the adoption of the 'eightfold path' towards nirvana. According to Mahayana Buddhism we might be aided by a Bodhisattva who, out of compassion, delays his path to nirvana in order to show us the way. Nevertheless, salvation is an individual affair, something that we achieve for ourselves, precisely by ceasing to be ourselves, entering the condition in which there is no self to be.

Parsifal is not a Bodhisattva, helping Amfortas along the path to extinction. His compassion is not the renunciation of the *self*, as preached in the *Wisdom Sutras* of the Buddhists, but the affirmation of the *other*, as preached in the Gospels. For Parsifal the goal is to rescue the other, by taking on the other's suffering and so existing all the more fully in this world, straying, struggling, bewildered, but guided by love. This surely is what is Christian in the philosophy of *Parsifal*: the idea of a love that gives but does not take.

The gospels use the term *agapē* for this kind of love, which is to stand higher than the *erōs*, *storgē* and *philia* (loves based on sex, family and friendship) recognized by the Greek philosophers (see John 15:13). But there is a real question as to whether *agapē* can fully supply our emotional need. There is a longing in the human heart for an *existential* tie of love, one that binds one person to another in a relation of absolute affirmation and mutual support. Family love is like that, so too is erotic love. Such forms of love enable individuals to venture out into the world, knowing that they tread on firm ground. Hence they are the paradigms of love as this has been discussed, for example, by Simon May.[16] According to May the object of my love is the one in whom I search for the ground of my being, the one who promises to affirm my right to exist and to provide the reason for being what I am. By contrast, the love advocated in the Christian gospels, *agapē*, may seem more like an accidental tie, a relationship of goodwill that is offered equally to the stranger and the friend. It offers to the recipient no special confirmation of his value, and no special commitment to protect him against the world. How, then, can it offer a path to redemption, comparable to that metaphysical homecoming, that melting into each other, which is the promise (for Wagner at least) of the true erotic tie?

Agapē forms the substance of the second of the two great commandments issued in Leviticus and repeated by Christ, the commandment to love your neighbour as yourself. Indeed, it was described by Kant as 'the love to which we are commanded'. But can love really be commanded? The Vulgate translation of *agapē* is *caritas*, and in European languages the word 'charity' has acquired impersonal, even somewhat derogatory connotations, precisely because charity is commanded. (Hence the proverbial expression 'cold as charity'.) The object of charity may be a duty; but the object of *agapē* is also an inspiration – a person whose receipt of a gift is itself a gift to the giver. On this view the Saviour's love was to bind us all in a new kind of fellowship, in which the conventional duty of mutual aid was replaced by heartfelt loving kindness – yet loving kindness conceived also as a duty, as the object of 'thou shalt'. It is the particular other, the one who feels and suffers, who is the true object of *agapē*, and this love is a source of consolation both to the one who receives it and to the one who gives. What is given might be seen as 'charity' in the legalistic sense – i.e. as given to this particular person under a general description that others too could satisfy – but it is given in another spirit, namely to this person in himself, *de re* and not *de dicto*.

The New Testament epistles wrestle with this idea, which is at the root of an innovative theology. In the well-known passage in 1 John 14:6 it is said that God is *agapē*, and who lives in *agapē* lives in God, and God in him. Through *agapē* we do not merely embrace the other person, we embrace and are embraced by God. It is because God loves us in this way that we, too, are capable of such love. We do not obey the second of Christ's commandments, therefore, simply by offering help to others according to a book of rules, as though love were a tax on income and the neighbour a merely abstract beneficiary. We obey the commandment by taking the particular person to heart and offering in our own way the kind of assurance that God offers through his love. Seen in that way *agapē* begins to look more like an existential than an accidental tie: and also more like a *calling*. (The theme of the calling penetrates the original Grail literature, a complement to the theme of the quest.)

But of course we cannot pour out love to everyone at every moment. If we are to care for the particular person as God cares for us, we must pay attention to those nearest to us, and try to care for them as individuals, which means consoling, cherishing, sharing their interests and feelings as our own. That is the work of sympathy (*Mitleid*). A charitable person can give to many causes, do good at every turn, but be devoid of sympathy, withdrawing from every individual call to console and cherish. Indeed, the Kantian ideal of moral rectitude requires precisely that we be motivated by law and not by sympathy, and the less the sympathy the more commendable the act. For Kant neighbour-love was a form of respect for each other and for the moral law that governs us. He dismissed the ethic of sympathy, since it makes the motive of morality *pathological* (i.e. a passion rather than a rational choice). The 'very feeling of compassion and tender sympathy, if it precedes the deliberation on the question of duty and becomes a determining principle, is even annoying to right thinking persons, brings their deliberate maxims into confusion, and makes them wish to be delivered from it and to be subject to law-giving reason alone'.[17]

Kant's passionate defence of his passionless morality is one of the marvels of philosophy, deriving the finest psychological distinctions and the highest aspirations with an equal logic from the idea of an impartial and emotionless law. The philanthropist with abundant resources might live by that law and flatter himself that he is exhibiting the 'love to which we are commanded', even though his heart is cold, and he is moved in no other way by the sight of suffering. By contrast, the sympathetic person may have neither the resources nor the knowledge to do good more widely than to the one in immediate need, but he is the one who lives by *agapē*, and who is the true disciple of Christ.

There is an interesting contrast here between two possible readings of Christ's parable of the Good Samaritan, given in answer to the question: 'Who is my neighbour?' The orthodox reading tells us that Christ was telling us to ignore distinctions of ethnicity and faith, and to do good to others in an impartial and universal way. But there is another, and in my view more plausible reading, according to which the Samaritan finds himself confronted with a *specific* obligation to a *specific* person. His assistance is offered in response to an individual need; it is not a contribution to the sum of the good, but an obligation to a fellow human being whose evident need is also an appeal for help. Having undertaken this obligation the Samaritan then recognizes that it is not fulfilled merely by first aid. After transporting the victim to an inn and paying for his succour there, the Samaritan returns to see how he is getting on. He undertakes a concrete commitment, and recognizes that he must see the matter through. His duty of care has turned from law to love, from obedience to a commandment, to an identity of interests, and a breaking down of the barrier between self and other.

Christians strive to believe in this new kind of love as a genuine care for the other, while accepting that it is also a duty. 'Only when it is a duty to love,' wrote Kierkegaard, 'only then is love everlastingly secured against despair.'[18] All other forms of love, Kierkegaard added, are mediated by partiality, and are therefore exclusive; neighbour-love, by contrast, is impartial and therefore inclusive. It is precisely this that is most difficult in the duties that lie upon a Christian, the duty to love the other without loving in him some projection or remnant of the I: the duty of self-abnegation. 'In earthly love and friendship,' Kierkegaard wrote, 'partiality is the middle term. In love of the neighbor, God is the middle term . . . if a man loves his neighbor in one single other man, then he loves all men.'[19]

Some writers strive to make sense of this by arguing that the duty to love your neighbour as yourself is simply a corollary of the first commandment (the commandment to love God entirely), since what you love in loving your neighbour is the image of God in him. What that image amounts to in the soul of Hitler, Stalin or Pol Pot can reasonably be questioned. It seems easier to retreat to the position of Dostoevsky, and to see neighbour-love merely as a project, a way of blowing on the embers that lie dark in all of us, in the hope that a spark of God might glow.[20] But we know too that the spark can be lit. Sister Helen Prejean's account of the *agapē*-love between her and a murderer on death row shows the 'work of love' at its most poignant, bringing a sinner to confession, remorse and neighbour-love, so as to want forgiveness and to die in the hope of it.[21]

Such cases are exceptional, and exactly what the duty to love amounts to in ordinary life remains one of the troubling questions left in the world by Christ. It is not surprising that the life of *agapē* has been thought to require, in its exemplary version – the version from which we ordinary people learn – a special kind of community. And in that community the other and competing loves – attachment, friendship and *erōs* – tend to be controlled, fenced off or excluded. Hence *agapē* leads of its own accord to the vows of poverty, chastity and obedience. In a community shaped by those vows the monks and nuns can pursue 'works of love', in Kierkegaard's words, free from earthly passions. Such was the Order of Knights Templar and such, presumably, was the original intention of Titurel, in founding the Order of the Grail.

Nor is this idea of the religious community, isolated from the normal modes of human intimacy, peculiar to Christianity. The teachings of the Buddha are addressed to the members of such a community. Even if the rest of the world is expected to imitate the course that the Buddha recommends, it is 'monks' whom he addresses. The *sangha*, the monastic community, is one of the three jewels that the Buddhist must treasure in his heart, and is the proof that all can live in another way. For the Buddhist the world of *samsara* has no sovereignty, since we carry within ourselves the image of another and purer community than the one that encumbers us in our daily lives. In the same way St Paul addresses his brothers and sisters in Christ, urging them to form communities of the faithful, and to turn away from *erōs*, marrying, if at all, only as a defence against sin. The religious order arises precisely from the attempt – shared by Christianity, Buddhism and the Sufis – to shape *agapē* as an existential tie, a bond of love on which individuals can rely for their validation because united thereby to 'the eternal in man'.[22] The pollution of the chaste order by sexual passion became, in due course, one of the themes of European anti-clerical literature, coming to an extraordinary climax in Diderot's brilliant novel *La Religieuse* (c. 1780).

All those thoughts must be borne in mind when considering the nature of Parsifal's calling. As I have argued, the religious devotion of Monsalvat is not founded on the hope for eternal life. There is a benefit sought by the Grail's devotees, but it is a benefit here and now, in the transformed consciousness of those who partake in the ceremony. This transformed consciousness ought also to be a renewal of *agapē*, and the recurring question at the heart of the drama is whether it can really be such a thing. Christ's death on the cross offered a transcendent sympathy, an inwardness with all that suffers which is strong enough to take the highest suffering on itself and to serve thereby as an example to the rest of us, through which we may consecrate our lives. But the Eucharist of the Grail temple involves the pitiless torture of Amfortas. The Redeemer's compassion is remembered in a ceremony that is in itself entirely devoid of it. This is one aspect of the deep disorder that reigns in the kingdom of the Grail.

Schopenhauer wrote that 'all true, pure love is compassion, and all love that is not compassion is selfishness; selfishness is *erōs*, compassion is *agapē*.'[23] We may not go so far as Schopenhauer in opposing *agapē* and *erōs* completely,[24] but the distinction between them is deep, and provides the theme of the second Act of Wagner's drama. There can be abusive and destructive *erōs*, but not abusive and destructive *agapē*. If we look at the growth of love in the human soul we will surely recognize that, *pace* Freud, *erōs* does not precede our first attachments, even if it may sometimes issue from them. Love between mother and child is founded in sympathy and need: indeed, the child's love for the mother is an example of what C. S. Lewis calls 'need love', love that arises from existential attachment, rather than the other way round.[25] The desire to protect and cherish is passed to the child, whose first loves beyond parents and siblings are dolls, soft toys and appealing animals. And this brings us to a profound observation at the heart of the *Parsifal* story, which is that the compassionate core of *agapē* does not extend only to other persons, but reaches into the animal kingdom too. *Erōs*, properly understood, extends only to another person, only to the one who can say 'I'. Like incest and paedophilia, bestiality is a pollution, a mixing of things that it is forbidden to mix, a violation of the 'natural' order, by which is meant the order in which persons are free and accountable beings, in right relation with their kind. (Bestiality is precisely an escape from the vision of the other that Sartre identifies as the core of desire: the vision of the other as 'transcendence'.)

Agapē extended to an animal excites no similar revulsion. Our feelings towards animals exhibit the sympathy that is the heart of *agapē* in all its forms. We cannot, Aquinas argues, feel friendship towards a horse, since that involves a reciprocal and enquiring concern for each other's interests; but we can certainly feel affection, sympathy and compassion.[26] Parsifal's first moral lesson at Monsalvat is learned from the death of the swan that he has shot, whose fate is dramatized by Gurnemanz. This scene, developed from a hint or two in Wolfram's *Parzifal*, is decisive for understanding not only the role of compassion in the story, but also the nature of the *agapē* that grows from it, an emotion that is pure giving, and which asks for nothing in return.

Wagner's love of animals and his championship of laws that would protect them (notably from vivisection) are well known. Like Schopenhauer he regarded our stance towards animals as a test of our moral sincerity: to offer kindness where there is no reward, not even the reward of gratitude, is to escape from selfishness and to renounce the dominion of the self-affirming will. Gurnemanz's description of the swan is of a creature that is not just an instance of the species but a particular bird with a life of its own. Compassion for the swan quickly turns to grief at its death and thence to a moment of mourning. And this recalls those commendable feelings in children, when they take some animal to heart and wish to protect it from injury. This is the primordial moment of cherishing. Compassion takes on the burden of another life, not in some rule-governed and 'virtue-signalling' way, but because this life is my life, and it and I are one. Such, according to Schopenhauer, is the meaning of the Vedic injunction that 'you are that thing' – *tat tvam asi*.[27] And in witnessing the agony of Amfortas Parsifal likewise 'becomes that thing', knows of his one-ness with Amfortas, at the very moment when Amfortas is compelled by the knights of the Grail, yet again, to pay the price of their communion, which is also the price of his sin.

Wagner believed that the suffering of animals is in some ways more terrible than that of human beings, since 'for an animal there is no element of reconciliation in suffering.'[28] Like the Redeemer, a human being can make a gift of his suffering, say to himself and to the other that it is *for your sake* that I suffer this. In this way a human being can rise above suffering, show that it is subordinate in the scheme of things to the compassion that it invites. He can bring suffering into the sphere of the I/Thou encounter, seeing it as a condition for which there is a reason and not just a cause. Suffering can in this way form a connection, a way of sharing, which joins people together in a work of love.

As Martha Nussbaum has pointed out, in an important discussion, the Stoics condemned compassion not only as a weakness, but also as an offence against the equal dignity of human beings.[29] Compassion is condescension, so the Stoics thought, and this view endures both in Kant's morality of interpersonal respect, and in Nietzsche's less temperate embrace of the Stoic virtues. The view would have some plausibility, if we thought of compassion merely as pity. It is precisely for this reason, however, that compassion needs to be incorporated into the ethic of *agapē*. For *agapē*, compassion is the occasion for love, not condescension. This love involves reaching out to the other in a posture of self-giving. There can be no condescension in this, no 'charity' in the cold-blooded, rule-guided sense of the term. That surely is what is at stake in Parsifal's calling. He has been called to the rescue of another individual, to suffer that individual's temptations and to recuperate what once the other lost. At no point does he look down on Amfortas as lower in the scheme of things than himself. On the contrary, there is an absolute equality of being between them. *Agapē* lifts compassion above condescension, by creating an existential bond.

Titurel was a noble and spiritual hero, fit recipient of the Grail, and the honest Gurnemanz vouches for this. Nevertheless Titurel is also part of the disorder of Monsalvat as we witness it in Act I. His selfish insistence on yet another spell of life, indifferent to the suffering of his son, even relishing it as a justified punishment, is a symbol of the way in which the love promised in the Eucharist has by now evaporated. Without the element of compassion the love of neighbour is no more than law, and mere procedures replace the warm recognition of the other, as the one whose fate you share. In the aftermath of Kundry's kiss, however, discovering in himself the real source of Amfortas's pain, Parsifal's knowledge extends beyond Amfortas, to the Grail community itself, and to the holy relics entrusted to its care.

It was not only Amfortas who cried out to the fool for rescue: it was the sanctuary itself, crying 'Erlöse, rette mich aus schuldbefleckten Händen!' – redeem me, rescue me, from guilt-tainted hands. It is not clear here whether it is the Grail that is crying for release from the tainted hands of Amfortas, or the Spear, from the far more tainted hands of Klingsor. Maybe it doesn't matter. Maybe we should understand Parsifal's new insight as extending to comprehend the full danger that had engulfed Amfortas, and which threatened the spiritual project that he held in trust. As I argued in Chapter 2, the tightly woven music of this episode, which sheds a penetrating light on Parsifal's inner feelings, shows that the 'torment of love' is not a threat only to Amfortas and Parsifal. It is a threat to the Saviour himself, whose message of sympathy has been obliterated by the passions stirred by those guilt-stained hands.

So what does the religion of Monsalvat achieve and why do the knights so tenaciously cling to it? Rituals and mysteries are pursued for no earthly purpose; they include all who share the bond of membership, and they enable the participants to set their competitive struggles aside in order to focus instead on their shared devotion to the gods. It is not the existence of the gods that makes this possible, but the unquestioning belief in the distinctions that they authorize, between the sacred and the profane, the pure and the polluted, those included in the communion and those excluded by some error or transgression. Events on which the long-term well-being of society depends – copulation, birth, death, war – come wrapped in just such religious conceptions. And those conceptions shape the psyche of believers, by putting them in direct contact with all those, whether living, dead or unborn, who are members of the group, joined in communion with the faithful.

That way of seeing the place of religion in the human community was famously elaborated by Émile Durkheim.[30] It sees religion from outside, not crediting either the truth of its doctrines or the consolation of its rites. Wagner has such a theory too, and he anticipates Durkheim, just as he anticipates Lévi-Strauss, Frazer, Girard and Douglas. But he portrays religion in *Parsifal* from the *inside*, in terms of the beliefs and conceptions of its devotees. There are two questions, therefore, that are prompted by the climax of the drama: what does Wagner mean by 'redemption', and what do his characters understand by that word; for instance, when singing of 'redemption to the Redeemer'? (Or is it redemption only to 'the redeemer'? All nouns have an initial capital in German, whether or not they are also names.)

I suggest that we are redeemed when the taint of wrong relations is washed away, when we can rejoin the community, freely accepting and accepted, able to lead a new life without sin. To achieve this condition we depend on those who can heal our wounds, who can perform the priestly office of retrieving, from the dark places of humiliation, the precious part of ourselves that was then severed from us. The outgoing part of us, the will that seeks to imprint the trials and triumphs of individuality on the world, once ventured forth, only to fall into sin. Redemption does not consist, as it consists for Schopenhauer, in the renunciation of the will, but in the recuperation of the will from tainted relations, and its return to a life of *agapē*.

This work of recuperation cannot be achieved alone. *Agapē* comes to us from others, and in particular from the great examples of compassion. This is what it means to say that we are redeemed by a redeemer. Compassion lifts the burden of woe from our shoulders and enables us once again to stand firm in the life of the community, confident in the example we have received. The one who heals in that way tends to come into the community from outside: the redeemer is ignorant of the conventions and compromises, the worn excuses of the Pharisees; and he is appalled by the way in which things are held precariously together by the constant sacrifice of victims. Through compassion this fool sees past all the fudges and self-flattery whereby we govern our lives, to the underlying battle with evil. We ourselves have lost that battle, though we deceive ourselves that it no longer needs to be fought. He, however, is able to engage in it and win it on our behalf, helping us to purge the inheritance of abusive relations and to return to the works of love.

The great weakness in the old story of the Grail was the assumption that pity would be enough, that it sufficed to show interest in another's tragic condition, to ask the question 'What ails you?', and the whole moral and metaphysical disorder of the Grail kingdom would be rectified. When Wagner said to King Ludwig that he had 'dispensed with the question' it was by way of rejecting that vision of compassion, as a pitying interest in another's misfortune.[31] He wished instead to be true to the underlying story of the innocent outsider, the one whose compassion is more than pity, precisely because it is a discovery of the other, leading to a discovery of the self. In this way compassion is a way of learning the deep truth about the moral world, the truth that other people are essentially connected to us, and if salvation is to come to us, it must come through them. Sin is a kind of existential loneliness, an eclipse of the other by the self – the state of mind expressed in Kundry's sexual passion and in Klingsor's exultant tyranny.

In place of the question Wagner gives us the Spear, one of the two holy relics entrusted to the Grail knights, which Amfortas has caused to be desecrated. Allegorical meanings congregate around these relics and it is no part of Wagner's intention at the end of the drama to disentangle them: on the contrary, the conclusion offers us a tight knot of significance, which it is impossible to untie completely. But we should note that the Spear was never a weapon in the hands of the Redeemer. In taking it as a weapon to the fight against Klingsor, Amfortas had already abused it. The Spear became a weapon in the hands of Klingsor because Amfortas had intended it to be a weapon of his own. He had failed to understand that this relic owes its sacred character not to the one who wielded it, but to the one who received it in his side, thereby giving his blood in atonement for our sins. Parsifal, in retracing Amfortas's path, is careful never to use the Spear as a weapon. It is to be returned to its true significance, as an instrument of the Passion, rather than an instrument of war. The Redeemer taught us to forgive our enemies, to love those that hate us, and most of all not to fight evil with the weapons that evil might use. By rescuing the Spear from this abuse, using it only to make the sign of the cross, Parsifal returns it to its true nature, as an instrument of healing.

True compassion is not reducible to a mechanical forgiveness, an acceptance of the sinner despite his fault. True compassion means accompanying the other back to the source of his wound, suffering all the doubt and insecurity associated with his humiliation. It involves rectifying not a momentary peccadillo, but an existential fault, a wrong turning that cannot be corrected without a gift of love. The life of compassion is far lonelier, therefore, than the life of erotic love. You must wander in self-doubt, knowing that the victim will not offer the equivalent of what he receives when the burden is lifted. This essential loneliness of the life of compassion is portrayed in the Prelude to Act III of Wagner's opera, and in the remorse that Parsifal feels, when reflecting on the delays and misfortunes that have encumbered his path.

Kundry, Amfortas, Gurnemanz and Parsifal do not take an anthropological perspective on their own condition: they obey imperatives framed in the language of faith. Amfortas has abused the sacred relics, failing to understand their peace-giving nature. He has polluted the shrine at which the community renews itself, and the wine of communion flows only when his wound is opened and his blood flows too. He sees the shrine of the Grail as desecrated by his presence, and he longs for death, the only secure and lasting relief from moral and physical torment. But the Redeemer to whom he prays will not grant him that relief, cannot grant it, because he no longer exists. He came and he went, leaving only the gift of his suffering, the lasting trace of which is contained in the Grail.

In all this it is clear that the relics must be revived by a purely human sympathy. It is only if another person takes Amfortas's suffering into himself that the wound will close, for 'Die Wunde schliesst der Speer nur, der sie schlug' (the wound is closed only by the Spear that struck it), and, being wounded, Amfortas cannot set out in search of the Spear. Is the Redeemer the author of this unforgiving punishment? Not exactly, for the Redeemer's only fault is to exist as a memory and not as a fact. It is for us to keep that memory alive, to rehearse in a spirit of discipleship all that the Redeemer did when he made a gift of himself – only then will we experience the spiritual healing that the Grail and its ritual promise, which is the return to right relations with our kind. This is the thought contained in those enigmatic closing words: 'redemption to the Redeemer'. The one referred to is both the original Redeemer and the one who rescues Him, the redeemer of the shrine who is redeemed in turn by his act of redemption. The trace left by the Redeemer can now do the Redeemer's work, which is to lead the knights along the path of real discipleship. All those many meanings are tied in the knot of the concluding words, which do not so much explain what has happened as wrap it in a single enigma.

In Chapter 2 I raised the question why the knights should persist in maintaining the sanctuary, and so forcing their king to conduct the ceremony that causes him exquisite pain. The answer to this question, I suggested, is to be found in the music, which shows that, for all the doctrinal uncertainty, the communion is a genuine act of consecration, a ceremony that really does 'make sacred' the shared life of its devotees. Such ceremonies cannot be simply abandoned; nor can they be replaced without a moral upheaval – a conversion of the whole community to another faith or another way of being. Such we witness in all the centuries of religious conflict and division, and this fact goes to the heart of religion. That which is sacred is, in Durkheim's words, 'set aside and forbidden': it cannot be changed or touched by profane hands and, like a precious casket, it contains within itself the shared life and the devotion unto death of the entire community. Atheists may take this to be a condemnation of religion. Wagner, by contrast, takes it to be an immovable part of our humanity. And if that is so, we must find the way to live with our religious need, to accept the call to the devout life, without making it into an instrument of torture.

Parsifal identifies with Amfortas's religious vision of himself, as condemned to suffer by his sin. He comes to understand the extent of his own sin, in abandoning his mother, in pursuing childish adventures rather than salvation, in relishing, however briefly, the kiss of Kundry, in toying with the *Qual der Liebe*, in straying from the path to Monsalvat into the waste land of sterile emotions. In so many ways he has betrayed his mission, which is to understand and fulfil the call of the Grail. It is through the birth of compassion that he is able to confront the difficulties before him, and return to Amfortas with the Spear. But in rescuing Amfortas he has restored the religious community, which can live once again the life of discipleship.

Gurnemanz witnesses the events from a position of faith, freed from temptation and naively trusting in the Grail's sacred prophecy. His is a consecrated life, the kind of life that is urged by the gospels, and he takes upon himself to consecrate Parsifal too, at last anointing him as king. In the personality of Gurnemanz we come to see how sacredness enters our world. Acts of sacrifice and consecration fill his days, and he sees the world as a revelation of holiness, which shines on him from the no-place of Monsalvat.

Kundry, caught between two worlds, lives outside the realm of *agapē*. Hence she can be captured by a spell, brought against her will into a realm where her will is redirected towards destruction. The work of destruction involves the desecration of what has been consecrated, and the pursuit of polluted pleasures. Her curse is lifted, however, and the spell broken; thereafter she can embark on the path of penitence – the renunciation of all desire, other than the desire for consecration. Redemption comes because she has tempted the one who sees into the depth of her being, who discovers in himself the turmoil that prevails in her, and understands her longing to be released from it. By lifting her, through baptism, into the realm of *agapē*, Parsifal brings her restless will to rest. Parsifal too is brought to rest, united with the source of spiritual nourishment, the trace left in this world by that never-to-be-repeated act of sacrifice, the example of which is all the redemption that we have or could hope to have.

All those characters grow in their diverse ways from the central predicament of *Parsifal*: and the role of the music is not merely to dramatize that predicament, but to express, by means of it, the unity and wholeness to which human life aspires. In the next chapter I will try to show how the music accomplishes that demanding task. In conclusion, however, we should not forget that there is another way of seeing *Parsifal* entirely: neither as a drama of extreme characters, nor as a religious parable, but as the story of Everyman. Such, perhaps, was Wolfram von Eschenbach's original intention. His story describes a quest – a journey in search of a treasure once glimpsed, and then lost through stupidity and ignorance. This trope survives in Wagner's version, but the quest is for something *inner*, for a triumph over weakness and temptation, as the hero shifts his attention from Self to Other, in an attempt to rectify the world.

On this interpretation, Parsifal enters Monsalvat as an innocent boy, deprived of social knowledge and without attachments apart from that to his mother, of whom he becomes properly conscious only when awoken by a stranger. Something like this is the condition of us all. We enter a world that has been endowed with meaning by others whom we do not know, and who have bound human life in mysterious rules and rituals. We are alone, with only one firm base from which to begin our explorations.

This firm base is the mother.[32] What we know of love we learn from her; but we learn it by osmosis rather than enquiry. The great transition, from receiving love to giving it freely, is something that we must earn. Not everyone achieves this transition, and the striving is fraught with trials, some painful, some delightful, all tainted by the world of spells and domination. All around us are the traces left by others in their search for power. And from the endless stream of suffering and conflict has issued a collective cry for rescue. The world that we enter is a world fraught with religious need. Its mysteries are man-made mysteries, which conceal the truth of our condition and obscure the path to redemption. The customs and rituals promise strength, community and renewal. But at their heart lies the inescapable fact of evil. The spirit of negation haunts the world of human relations, turning care to dominion and love to sexual hunger. The world into which we are born must therefore be rectified, and this is revealed in all the paths that we might take in our efforts to live as we should.

It is revealed in sexual love, in which we risk the loss of our autonomy, and subjection to another's control. It is revealed in our religious need, which tempts us to seek refuge in illusory ideas of communion. It is revealed in the adventures that lead us to stray from the path of compassion, and in compassion itself, which tempts us into helpless pity, diverting us from the real task, which is to take the burden of another's suffering on ourselves.

And somewhere in the background is another narrative entirely, the story of a redeemer, who once made a gift of his suffering, so as to refashion it as love. The story of this redeemer haunts our days, even if we have no knowledge of who he is, why he came, or whence he has departed. The solution to the mystery comes only when we understand that his story is our story, and that we ourselves are the redeemer. We have been called not to explore the world, but to rescue it. In doing so we emerge from our trials and conflicts in full possession of our social nature. Like the Redeemer, we make a gift of our suffering, through an act of consecration that brings peace to us all. Whether or not there is a God, there is this hallowed path towards a kind of salvation, the path that Wagner described as 'godliness'. That is the path taken by Parsifal, and it is a path that is open to us all.

5

The Music

The sound-world of *Parsifal*, issuing from Wagner's astonishing
melodic and harmonic imagination, is also *sui generis*. Although it
was the last work that he wrote, it has the sound of a discovery, as
though a door had opened in the composer's soul on to a fresh, varied
and abundant musical landscape that had never been visited before.
Tristan passes by chromatic voice-leading from one unresolved dissonance to the next, seldom pausing on a triadic consonance as it
moves restlessly between competing tonal centres. Chromatic voice-
leading, in which the voices move through consecutive semitones, is
omnipresent in *Parsifal* too, but it tends to generate consonant triadic
harmonies, which pass enharmonically from key to key. Indeed, this
has a fair claim to be a hallmark of the *Parsifal* language.

Parsifal, like the earlier mature works, uses leitmotifs that gather
meaning as the score unfolds. However, the theme with which the
work begins is not a leitmotif, but a complete melody from which
leitmotifs are subsequently extracted, in a process that is unique to
Parsifal. This melody I have called, following Derrick Everett, the
Grundthema (1), and Wagner said that the rest of the music unfolds
from it, as a flower from its bud.[1]

Although that is not entirely true, the *Grundthema* immediately
impresses the listener with its weight of meaning. It is like the opening theme of a Bruckner symphony, a huge statement of intention,
standing at the front of the work like the ceremonial entrance to a
temple. Sounding unaccompanied, in unison, and staying off the beat
for two bars, it invokes the measureless rhythm and unison cadences
of plainsong; and the poignant phrases that are later to be associated
with sin and suffering, while seamlessly bound within its contours,
seem ready to break away and grow on their own. The melody is at

once repeated, behind a shimmering veil of orchestral sound, creating an unforgettable impression of prayerful yearning. A more piercing icon of the religious way of life, poised between hope and sorrow, could hardly be imagined, and when the *Grundthema* has again sounded twice, this time in its minor version (1A), the listener can only be thankful that it is succeeded by a moment of silence, anticipating several other such moments in a work that again and again takes contrition to the limit, raising imploring hands to a Heaven that seems never to reach down in return.

The leitmotifs, including those subsequently extracted from the *Grundthema*, are not, on the whole, onomatopoeic in character; nor are they storytelling devices. Their content is largely mental, connected with feelings and ideas, rather than specific objects. Faith, suffering, guilt, atonement, woe, redemption – these are the aspects of our world that are most tightly woven into the musical fabric, by melodies and harmonies that are saturated with the inner life. Even when there is something concrete that a leitmotif 'stands for', it is only by way of dissolving that thing in the flow of ambient emotion. Thus the Grail motif, adapting the Dresden Amen (2),[2] so self-contained and statuesque in itself, like a divinely given guarantee, appears in that aspect only rarely. For the most part it emerges from the musical flow with the force of an aspiration, like a ray of sunlight through clouds, often distorted and dimmed by the enharmonic substitutions that I describe below. The Klingsor motif (18), so suggestive of malice and destruction, crystallizes from the slime of sorcery, as though the character were no more than a temporary form adopted by a larger, world-destroying force.

Parsifal's motif (21), redolent at first of the free life in the forest, develops as the boy develops, until emerging in full sovereign authority when the boy becomes king. Kundry's outlandish cry (11), sounding from some place of nightmares, tears the fabric of Monsalvat, revealing darkness and destruction behind the veil of pious ritual. Thus, when Amfortas, in deepest contrition, cries out for mercy before the Grail, the Grail motif, searching for its resolution, slips and slides through conflicting keys, until tumbling into the abyss from which Kundry screams:

As in *Tristan*, the music does not come to a sudden halt in order to allow the leitmotif to be stated. The motif appears in the course of things, a natural outgrowth of the musical development, in just the way that a thought is sparked off in the flow of ordinary experience and then submerged by it. In almost all the important cases, the leitmotif is precipitated out of the musical movement, of which it forms an integral and often culminating part. By emerging in this way from the musical argument, motifs acquire a unique kind of intensity, as though they have burst through the surface, bearing messages from elsewhere. In *Parsifal* this effect is especially vivid on account of the solemn and poignant nature of so much of the material, which sounds with the voice of an observing consciousness, following the drama from a place outside the action. When motifs like those of the wound (4) and the Spear (5) glow through the musical line, it is as though the musical fabric becomes suddenly transparent, revealing an order of events far greater than anything that we observe on stage. This constant slipping from *chronos* to *kairos* is fundamental to the *Parsifal* vision of the human condition.

Some of the repeated melodic and harmonic elements of *Parsifal* are mere phrases, absorbed into the texture of other and larger ideas. Such is true of the short chromatic phrases associated with yearning and pleading (38A and B), and the diatonic caresses of the flowermaidens (31A and B). But the critical material – the material that bears the full emotional weight of the drama – consists of complete blocks of sound, in which melodic elaboration is wound together with harmonic networks and rhythmic emphasis. Two examples of this – the 'cries of woe' (*Wehelaute* – the term is von Wolzogen's (25)), and the motif of the prophecy (*der Reine Tor* (9)) – will serve as illustrations.

The first conveys suffering, yearning and guilt in a way that touches on all the woe of the world, and whose melodic and harmonic devices are recalled and embellished in so many situations in the drama.[3] In its agonized and most stressful form, as it bursts through the tissue of the transformation music in Act I, the cry sounds like a communal appeal for salvation. But in its muted and incomplete variants it rains on Monsalvat like tears of a general sorrow. In its muted variants it is a fragment of a descending chromatic scale:

But it is very much more than a scalar fragment. The parallel thirds suggest people clinging to each other in their sorrow, while the marching bass line urges them onwards, as though for ever:

Into the heart of this solemn texture Wagner inserts the real melody of the motif, derived ultimately from the concluding phrase of the *Grundthema* in its minor version, 1A:

And on that hand-wringing gesture Wagner then superimposes, in the crucial moment of the transformation music, a scalar and arpeggiated passage for violins that seems to tear itself apart in frenzy:

The combination of those four elements, filled out with as many subsidiary figures as the whole will bear, is one of the most unforgettable icons of imploring sorrow in the whole of music. Notice, however, that it does not depart from a strict tonal organization, the bass moving around the circle of fifths in a sequence that recalls Bach at his most majestic. In this bass line, indeed, we hear the message of eternal return, of the impregnation of sorrow into all else that we are, joy and sacredness included.

Things are otherwise with the prophecy motif (9), which deals with tonal relations in a way that is perhaps peculiar to *Parsifal*. Here are the first four bars of the motif that immediately follow the scene with the flower-maidens:

This sequence, variously extended or contracted, is the heart of the motif. The phrase that completes it, which occurs only twice, is, like the accompanying words, a feeble addition, resolving everything with a naive IV-I cadence in the major (which would be C major in the instance quoted). Not surprisingly, Wagner chose to leave the completing phrase (9B) to one side, and to take the melodic sequence of fifths (full and diminished), with its accompanying harmonic network, as the true statement of Parsifal's future identity.

The chord in the first bar contains all the notes of the E flat major scale save the tonic and the dominant, while the chord in the second bar contains *only* those two notes, apart from the tied G in the bass. The result is a quite novel sense of progression. There is no way of parsing the first chord through the conventions of common practice harmony, and those conventions are in any case violated by the second chord, composed of an open fifth, emphatically doubled. But the transition from the first chord to the second has a startled quality, like someone wiping his hand across his forehead, and suddenly seeing clearly what before was veiled in doubt.

Sequences like this occur in *Tristan*, propelled by chromatic voice-leading, along paths of consecutive semitones. In the prophecy motif too there is chromatic movement in the alto voice, using a version of the pleading/yearning motifs that I have numbered 38A and 38B. But this fragment of voice-leading is not what gives definition to the progression. We find here a new way of extracting chords from the diatonic scale and then moving between them.

In *Tristan* each harmony is dissolved in the continual chromatic flow, creating an order quite distinct from traditional chord grammar. There is a similar chromatic flow in *Parsifal*, not through unresolved dissonances as in *Tristan*, but from one consonant triad to another, creating rapid enharmonic substitutions that establish no real change of key. The semitone movements between the voices often create 'hexatonic cycles' – harmonies that move by semitone voice-leading through a circle of triads, involving the notes of a hexatonic scale. Richard Cohn has associated this form of enharmonic movement with the attempt to portray 'uncanny' events in opera and song.[4] It is worth noting, in particular, the way in which the Grail motif, based on a simple and stable-seeming IV-I cadence, is constantly dissolved by chromatic voice-leading and reassembled as a sequence of unrelated triads. Two instances will illustrate the point. First, when Parsifal, following the shock of Kundry's kiss, recalls the holy vessel's appeal for rescue, we hear this:

Then, as Parsifal ascends the steps of the altar at the end, so as to reveal the Grail, we hear this:

The successive triads of E flat major, B minor, G major, E flat minor and D flat major wash the scene in consonance, while erasing any suggestion of tonal grammar, as though we have stepped out of everyday succession into a moment in *kairos* time. Shortly afterwards the Grail theme is stated in A flat, but with an A minor triad replacing the B flat minor that ought to guide the motif to its conclusion. In this striking substitution the whole drama seems to resound, and at this moment Kundry sinks dead to the ground. Somehow the music conveys the uncanny thought that she has been dead all along, which in a sense she has.

This use of enharmonic substitutions has been the topic of penetrating commentary from Richard Cohn and David Lewin.[5] They make clear the extent to which the euphonious sound of Wagner's score, with its moments of super-saturated consonance, is in fact something else, a way of using triads as independent musical entities, wandering constantly away from the keys that they define.

Given this triadic way of thinking the circle of fifths in the cries of woe above is heard as an immense intrusion into the score. Fifths play a distinctive role in *Parsifal*, sounding as though from far away, like the 'ancestral voices' of Coleridge. With the prophecy motif the fifths belong not in the bass but in the melody, and when the motif finally achieves full symphonic elaboration, as Parsifal tells Gurnemanz of his troubled journey to Monsalvat, it takes on a new life, melding together the fool, the Spear (5), straying (40), struggle (42) and the Grail (2) in a frenzy of parallel fifths (47). In these passages the interval of the fifth seems to be entirely emptied of its triadic content so as to become an entity in its own right.

Although voice-leading by semitone steps is fundamental to the enharmonic substitutions that occur everywhere in *Parsifal*, it is part of a distinctive chord grammar too. *Tristan und Isolde* opens with a chromatic motif leading to a famous chord, the 'Tristan chord' (A, transposed for clarity's sake at B in the example below), whose timbre and spacing seem to beg for the resolution that it never obtains. Seen as a chord – i.e. as a musical individual constructed vertically from its component pitches – it is by no means unfamiliar in the tradition of Western music, being a version of the half-diminished seventh (C), which in turn can be treated, in context, as a dominant ninth chord (D) without its root (middle C in this example):

By taking the half-diminished chord, C, and writing out its inversions, spacings and rival spellings we arrive at the catalogue of 'mystical' chords discussed by Alfred Lorenz, in the fourth volume of his treatise devoted to 'the secret of form' in the works of Wagner.[6] Lorenz, who was inspired by von Wolzogen's account of Wagner spending hours at the piano playing with novel harmonies, argues that the distinctive sound of a chord was as important to Wagner as its place, should it have one, in a wider syntax. And he explores the many ways in which versions and inversions of the half-diminished seventh appear in *Parsifal*, and are resolved there by standard harmonies. All the versions of C are, for Lorenz, 'mystical' chords.

However, A above is not, in *Tristan*, treated as an independent musical entity, whose meaning and effect can be grasped in isolation. It is the by-product of chromatic polyphony, inseparable from the voices that flow into it and away from it, leaving the chord as a kind of deposit in their wake, an image printed on the air. By contrast similar chords in *Parsifal* stand often free from any voice-leading, usurping the functions of more orthodox chords, and appreciated as sonorities in their own right.

The mystical chords are freestanding gestures, with a musical character that belongs to them as individuals, regardless of their place in any sequence. This can be clearly understood when the two chords that open *Tristan*, there understood as the deposits from chromatic voices, stand detached in *Parsifal*, as harmonizations of a melodic line over a chromatic bass:

Tristan:

Parsifal:

When such chords are combined in sequence with triads they give the effect of slipping off the edge, into a realm of darkness, as in Kundry's enchantment motif in which a half-diminished seventh arranged on the flattened sixth alternates with the dominant triad:

In *Tristan* chromatic voice-leading is the all-pervasive grammar of the work, the principle of connection that unites each note to its successor, and from which chromatic harmonies emerge as deposits along the way. In *Parsifal* the chromaticism of the sorcery motifs is a *departure* from triadic harmony, as in the example above, the momentary dissonance quickly washed away by a consonant triad. The ascending triad of the first bar is derived from the ascending triad that begins the entire work (1), though lingering on the chromatic accidental, A sharp, by way of challenging the tonal order. The chromatic harmony – a mystical chord, arranged so as to emphasize the flattened sixth – is 'resolved' on to a C major triad, while the second bar of the melody turns that triad to a dominant seventh by moving chromatically, so rescuing the A sharp (now B flat) as a normal participant in common practice harmony. We witness here the distinctive nature of chromaticism in Act II of *Parsifal*, as a voice-led movement between chords, here between a mystical chord and a triad. This is the equivalent in music of the malign sorcery in the drama. Chromaticism lasts only as long as the spell; and always, in the background, the world of triadic harmony is waiting to reassert itself – one reason why Act II returns constantly to the tonality of B minor, in which key it both begins and ends.

The 'mystical' chords sound very differently, depending on the spacing and distribution of the notes. Arranged as in the sorcery motif they point without strain to the chord that will resolve them. Elsewhere, however, they stand stark and resistant in the texture of the work. Throughout *Parsifal* we observe the great care with which Wagner attended to this matter, so that we are simultaneously aware of the rootless character of the chords, and of the way in which they stir the bass line on which they rest, as though brought into the music from somewhere outside its harmonic order. In this way the 'mystical' chords belong to a larger class of rootless sevenths, formed by excising the root from ninth chords built on the principles of diatonic harmony, all of which have a part to play in Wagner's lexicon. Here are some of them, from which the root, C, has been subtracted:

Rather than see the 'mystical' chords in Lorenz's way, therefore, as belonging to a single category of versatile semi-dissonances, it is better to understand them as part of a new tonal language – a language beyond that of *Tristan*, in which harmony issues from the free use of the scale, altered notes included, as in the first chord of the prophecy motif described above, together with the enharmonic substitutions that maintain the triad as a recurring unit of significance. In *Parsifal* all the triads are equals, and can occur at any moment, whatever the tonal centre of the score. Likewise all notes of the scale are equals, and all can enter any chord constructed on any of the scale degrees. Here, for instance, is part of the chord sequence that accompanies Klingsor as he exerts his grip on the newly awakened Kundry:

The effect of such a sequence is not one of fragmentation or dis-unity, but of a continual reaching out for something to grip, something that will hold us to the emotional story. The leitmotifs are thrown into relief, like knots in a rope across a swaying bridge. We hold on to them the more tightly, as the harmonies slip and slide beneath our feet. In Kundry's cry of 'Sehnen!', following on the passage above, every phrase comes from the Monsalvat lexicon and brings a meaning of its own to her desolation (see 11, 25A, 25B, 25C):

Kundry's cry of woe above the circle of fifths is all the more vivid and recognizable on account of the contrast with Klingsor's lawless chord-sequence, which is an exhalation from the abyss above which she sways, as she reaches in her desolation for the place that promised rescue.

The fourth volume of Lorenz's *Das Geheimnis der Form bei Richard Wagner* appeared in 1933. Lorenz was gripped by the extraordinary unity and organic wholeness of the Wagner masterpieces, qualities that seemed so hard to explain, given the free-flowing harmonies and the unashamed subordination of the music to emotional effect. Hence his obsessive need to catalogue the 'mystical' chords in all their per-mutations, as though calling a crowd of mischievous children to order before reciting their common practice catechism.

In a similar way Lorenz set out to discern a systematic order in the individual scenes, arguing that the traditional forms of medieval poetry survive in the Wagnerian dramas, uniting the music and the drama in tightly organized 'periods'. Two poetic structures in par-ticular interested Lorenz, the *Bar* form, AA'B (where A' may be a varied or developed form of A), and the *Bogen* (arch) form ABA. These forms are like the sonata form in classical music, governing the presentation, repetition and closure of musical and thematic ideas. Lorenz patiently took the Wagner operas apart, dividing them into periods in which one or other of those structures is shared by both the drama and the music, so explaining (to Lorenz's satisfaction at least) the extraordinary sense of unity exhibited by the work as a whole.

The inspiration for this approach comes from Wagner himself, who in *Opera and Drama* refers to the 'poetic-musical period' (*dichterisch-musikalische Periode*) – that is, a passage in which a single mood is developed musically – as the true unit of meaning in his dramas. Lorenz set out to discover such periods, and to identify each of them in terms of a tonal centre, a division into parts (usually *Bar* or *Bogen*), and a step-by-step correspondence between the dramatic action and the musical movement. However, the method is purely descriptive, rather like an academic account of key changes, and tells us nothing about the real inner unity of the music, or the sense of necessity that leads the musical movement onward from bar to bar. Although Lorenz makes an attempt to find a dramatic idea, and a musical movement, that characterizes each of his periods, the attempt misrepresents precisely what is most impressive about the form of *Parsifal*, which is the seamless flow of the music, unfolding from the opening *Grundthema*. Form, for the critic, is never a secret (a *Geheimnis*) but rather a vivid experiential fact, which needs only to be pointed out to be heard and enjoyed by the listener. With Lorenz's periodic structures and background tonalities, however, it is unclear that we are really being presented with what we hear, or ought to hear, in the music. The division of the work into periods often seems arbitrary, the result of the theory and not something experienced directly by the listener.

While few people accept Lorenz's particular way of dividing up the Wagner operas,[7] a movement has arisen among critics towards identifying background tonics and pitch-complexes sustained over long musical spans. Robert Bailey, Patrick McCreless, Reinhold Brinkmann and others have tried to substantiate Lorenz's basic intuition, that there is a hidden tonal order in Wagner's music, which unifies large time-spans by generating the musical surface by law-like procedures.[8]

Such suggestive accounts of Wagner's musical architectonic take us back to Heinrich Schenker, who believed that the masterpieces of classical music were all derived by the 'composing out' of a single 'background' cell, through 'middle ground' structures that generate the musical foreground.[9] This generative process involves harmonic and melodic transformations of a hidden *Ursatz*, itself a combination of perfect cadence and descending scale. Schenker represented his 'transformational grammar' in elaborate graphs that have exerted a fascination over musical scholarship in our times not unlike the fascination exerted by the Ptolemaic cosmology over medieval astronomers. Schenker himself did not believe that Wagner's wayward and chromatic musical argument could be subsumed under his theory – a fact that he regarded, characteristically, as condemning Wagner's music, rather than refuting his theory. Others, such as Brinkmann, Wintle and Bailey, have used Schenkerian graphs to trace stable 'middle grounds' in the extended passages that they have discussed. As I argue elsewhere, however,[10] these graphs should not be read as revelations of a 'hidden' order in the music, from which the audible surface is generated in some rule-governed way, but simply as critical tools, which may help us to hear more clearly the links that are there on the surface.

The only real dispute here is between those, like Carl Dahlhaus,[11] who believe that Wagner's 'poetic-musical periods' are relatively short, like the breaths taken in the course of the action, and those, like Lorenz and his followers, who think of them in the terms appropriate to a Brahms or Bruckner symphony, as extended musical arguments, in which material is presented and developed within a coherent tonal frame and with only extrinsic guidance from the drama. And both sides to this dispute are right: sometimes the periods conform to Dahlhaus's model, sometimes to Lorenz's. *Parsifal*, which begins and ends in A flat major, and which retains B minor as the background tonality throughout the second Act, yields fairly easily to the search for tonal centres and elaborately prepared modulations. But this is not what accounts either for the unity or for the emotional eloquence of the musical structure, both of which owe their being to Wagner's ability to synthesize musical and dramatic form, so that the music both leads the drama and is led by it, as in the unforced enharmonic modulation in the motif of love's sorcery, 16:

It is this interpenetration of musical and dramatic form that Wagner really had in mind, in referring to the 'poetic-musical period' as the building block of his works, and it is a feature that, far from being a 'secret', is immediately apparent to the ear.[12]

But how is the extraordinary sense of unity and wholeness achieved? This is where, it seems to me, we must leave all the alleged 'secrets' of the score behind us, and address the music as it is heard. We must attend to the way in which we hear themes and motifs emerge from a few central ideas, which are then pulled apart and recombined to create the fabric in which the whole and its parts are equally apparent, and equally full of meaning. Just as everything in *Tristan* unfolds from the opening melodic voices and the chord that crystallizes around them, so does nearly everything in *Parsifal* stem from the *Grundthema* (1) that launches the Prelude. The many fragments of this melody shine with a grisaille light on all the corners of the work, focusing the action in the perspective of a single observing eye. Suffering and relief, guilt and forgiveness, fragmentation and restoration are all connected, calling to each other across the three de-localized tableaus of the action. Through purely musical means Wagner shows the 'internal relation' that exists between sin and contrition, and between pollution and its cure.

The *Grundthema*, called the 'love-feast' motif by von Wolzogen, has three recognizable parts, each developed independently in the work as a whole and each acquiring, when taken alone, a distinctive character (A, B and C in the example):

Despite being the opening phrase of the entire work, A stays off the beat and rhythmically ambiguous until the very last note, by which time it has been overtaken by another motif, B, which is both anguished and assertive, with a pronounced and accented character (motif 4, sometimes known as the wound). A is in the key of A flat, the home key of the entire work, while B is in the key of the mediant, C minor, which, however, soon relinquishes its hold as fragment C takes over, returning the melody to the original key.

The three parts are themselves divided as the drama unfolds, A becoming the basis of the communion motifs and also, articulating a IV-I cadence, the motif of redemption (51). B is associated with pain, with the guilt of Amfortas, and also with Kundry's kiss, while C divides clearly in two, the rising figure being associated with the Spear (5A), and the falling, stumbling response (5B) with suffering and contrition, anticipating the *Wehelaute*, or cries of woe (25), the astonishing amalgam discussed above:

When the *Grundthema* is first sounded, unaccompanied and in unison, the multiple meanings have yet to be attached to its parts. Nor could they be so attached were it not for the evocative appeal, both of the parts themselves and of the melody as a whole. This opening melody visits the principal themes of the drama – communion, pain, transgression, sorrow and redemption – and combines them in an organic whole to which each part makes an indispensable contribution. The extraordinary relatedness of all that occurs in *Parsifal* is already present in this compelling auditory image, which stands at the threshold of the work replete with everything that follows. It is a fitting symbol both of the wholeness at which the religious way of life aims and of the conflicts contained in it, which must be suffered before they can be cured.

Of course, there is nothing remarkable in taking three or four melodic phrases and combining them in sequence as a single melody. Nor would it be remarkable to associate the component parts of that melody with disparate ideas, emotions and situations. What *is* remarkable, however, is the fact that the components of Wagner's melody develop in response to the situations that endow them with sense, and that they cling to each other when put together with an intense magnetic force, so as to demand the greatest harmonic strength to pull them apart again, as Wagner pulls them apart in the second half of the Prelude. The chemistry here is wholly intrinsic to the musical elements, which capture the meanings that accumulate around them and seem to reveal of their own accord that those meanings belong together. Sorrow, sin and redemption come into the world as one condition, calling for the sacrifice that will resolve the tension between them. The resulting musical unity is not just a symbol, but an *enactment* of the spiritual wholeness that is the object of Parsifal's quest.

The extraordinary fertility of the *Grundthema* is commented upon by Holloway, who notes that all the sub-motifs bracketed in this example are in play throughout the opera:

Some of the sub-motifs gain added poignancy when revisited in the C minor version of the *Grundthema*, which occurs immediately after the two initial statements in A flat major. This is especially true of the last sub-motif, which, in the minor version, becomes the motif of contrition (5B), amalgamated with that of suffering (6) to produce the heart-breaking 'commiserating sevenths' that coax the Prelude to its inconclusive conclusion.

Particularly remarkable in the minor version of the *Grundthema* is the phrase B, which, given the shift from A flat to the mediant, C minor, ought to be in E flat major, but which, by an altogether characteristic shift from the melodic to the harmonic minor scale, Wagner transposes to E minor, so doubling its poignancy, and preparing its return in the second part of the Prelude, infused then with all the pain and yearning that it will represent throughout the subsequent action:

What we witness in the Prelude is not the technically adept dismemberment of musical material. We witness musical form as Wagner had absorbed it from Beethoven, and Beethoven in turn from Haydn. A Beethoven theme will characteristically break down into motifs which can be developed independently, while retaining a musical appeal of their own, as well as a memory of the larger element from which they originate. His powerful way of reassembling and dramatizing melodic material was, as Wagner rightly saw, the true 'secret of form' in Beethoven's art, the source of the long-range thinking and orderly syntax that is also, at the same time, the highest expressive melody. To show that this is true of Beethoven is not part of my present purpose.[13] What is important is to see that Wagner is doing exactly the same kind of thing with the *Grundthema* in the Prelude. The theme is being treated as the source from which other motifs can be extracted so as to set off on paths of their own, each imbued with a musical character, and each attracting to itself an emotional ambience from the drama.

The subsequent life of the last phrase of the *Grundthema* is a case in point. It divides naturally into two, the first part associated with the Spear and the second with the lament and contrition of Amfortas. But each part acquires a character of its own as the drama unfolds. Once severed from each other they act like free radicals, pulled by the charge of other motifs, and amalgamating with them in ways that enhance not only their melodic depth, but also the emotional richness of their message. Already in the Prelude we hear the contrition motif adhering to the severed end of the motif of faith (3A), adding a kind of grieving dignity to the melody. As the drama unfolds, however, the motif of contrition hovers everywhere about the characters, clamping down on one phrase after another, and always with a radically transformative effect, as when Kundry, straining feebly against the psychological chains that imprison her, cries 'Ich will nicht Oh! . . . Oh!' before submitting to Klingsor's control:

Likewise with the Spear motif, 5A, which attaches to the beginning of other themes and motifs, generally as an up-beat, and which creates a sense of resolution and will, struggling against adversity, as in the Prelude to Act III.

The Beethovenian use of motifs as the building blocks of great arches of symphonic thought is not peculiar to Wagner. What is remarkable, and what plays a large part in creating the 'secret' of Wagner's form, is the role of these elements in the drama. The many fragments that can be lifted from the *Grundthema* are separately gripping as melodic phrases. When they sound in the orchestra during some critical moment they attract to themselves the emotional amb-ience of the stage, and translate it spontaneously into music. The musical valency of the motif infects the action with a similar valency, a yearning after the whole, as the first phrase (A) of the *Grundthema* yearns throughout the opera for the closure that comes with the final invocation of the Redeemer, and the up-beat of the Spear yearns towards the sorrowing cadence that brings it to rest. The yearning character of the phrase A is strikingly intensified in the wake of Kun-dry's kiss, when the F is flattened, the upward progress arrested, and the melody becomes a great cry in the void, without a resolution. This, the libretto tells us, is the cry of the Redeemer himself, the one who promised rescue, but who is himself far more deeply in need of it.

In *Tristan* the chromatic phrases melt into each other and flow onwards towards the all-extinguishing night. In *Parsifal*, by contrast, the leitmotifs reach out across the texture of the work for the motifs that will complete them, striving to find their place in a seamless totality that will include them all. This *musical* wholeness reflects the meaning of the work, which is the moral wholeness that we seek through the moment of religious submission – the incorporation of all that we are, passion, sin and suffering included, into the healed and restored con-dition by which we are reconciled to others and to ourselves.

In order to give musical embodiment to that moral idea Wagner put together his motifs from a small and adaptable lexicon. The *Grundthema* contains, in embryo, all the themes of worship, pain and contrition that are the soul of Monsalvat. The rising triad with which it opens, subject to chromatic alteration and 'mystical' har-mony, becomes the first part of Kundry's enchantment motif, from which the motif of Klingsor emerges by prolongation and octave dis-placement. Those two themes, together with the chromatic ties and half-diminished harmonies that stem from them, provide all the icons of domination and destruction in Klingsor's castle. The fifths and diminished fifths of the prophecy motif are echoed in the angular motif of desolation (39), while the motifs associated with the Grail, with Parsifal, with consecration and with the Good Friday meadows can all be mapped against the *Grundthema* in its final (redemption) version, revealing their audible diatonic resonance.[14] Wherever you look in *Parsifal* you find these cross-references woven into the fabric of the score. They are not 'hidden' or 'secret' devices, but plainly audible and gripping musical connections, which have the logic and inevitability, as well as the freedom and poignancy, of the links that bind the motifs in a Beethoven sonata-form movement.

Robin Holloway has presented a persuasive analysis of the main themes from the outer Acts of *Parsifal* that illustrates their unifying deep structure, showing them to be parallel exfoliations from the triad.[15] He summarizes the thematic interconnections in a 'slightly tongue in cheek ideogram (which puts all the music into the work's opening key of A flat for ease of comparison). It can be read left to right for musical line and story-line; and up and down for the vertical parallels that support the sense one has when listening that all this material is made out of the same diatonic shapes.'[16] Here is the ideogram, as Holloway presents it, and it surely speaks for itself:

What is most extraordinary about these parallels and reminiscences, however, is that they are not *merely* 'formal'. They illustrate the subject of the drama, showing, through a musical metaphor, how our innermost longings for healing contain within themselves the image of redemption, move of their own accord towards wholeness and completion, so that contrition and forgiveness, transgression and renewal belong together in the scheme of things, which is the scheme of our salvation.

6

The Principal Leitmotifs

There have been several distinguished accounts of the leitmotifs in *Parsifal*, including the original assignment of names by von Wolzogen, and the perceptive commentaries by Albert Lavignac and Maurice Kufferath.[1] Much of the critical heritage is summarized in the analytical catalogue produced by Derrick Everett, available on his Monsalvat website. I have added some suggestions of my own, and also adapted Everett's account in the light of my interpretation of the drama.

The following are the principal musical elements, roughly in the order of their appearance in the score. I have given them names where these have become established, and here and there suggested names of my own. The names are attempts to summarize the character and use of the leitmotifs, but are only a very approximate guide to what they signify in any particular context.

1. *Grundthema*. This is the apt name given by Everett to the haunting melody that opens the entire work. It is less a leitmotif than the source from which leitmotifs are extracted, in a manner that is distinctive of *Parsifal*:

1A. *Grundthema*, second version. This is a restatement of 1 in C minor (the key of the mediant), including a significant shift of tonal centre to E minor and an extension of the final cadence:

2. The Grail. This, adapted from the 'Dresden Amen' used in the Chapel Royal in Dresden, can be extended as here, so as to end on the dominant:

As the drama unfolds, the distinctive parallel sixths in this motif begin to assume a life of their own, recalling the Grail theme even when detached from it, while enharmonic substitutions for the triads produce distorted versions of the motif that flit, dream-like, behind and above the action.

3. Faith:

3A. Faith, grieving version, derived from 3 and the concluding cadence of 1A:

3B. Faith, exalted version, theme of the Dove:

4. The wound, pain, yearning. Extracted from the second and third bars of 1/1A:

5. The Spear. Extracted from the fourth bar of 1/1A:

5A. Contrition, sorrow; Kufferath: pity; the last two bars of 1A, emphasizing 5:

5B. Variant, without the Spear:

6. Suffering (extended variant of 5A):

7. Chivalry. A variant of 3, with a rhythmical prolongation:

Other versions of this occur in Gurnemanz's Act I narrative to the squires; for instance, when justifying Kundry ('Gut tut sie dann'), and when describing Titurel's founding of Monsalvat ('Titurel, der fromme Held'). The gift of faith (3) is a poised and static condition, but becomes active and outgoing in the life of chivalry, thus:

7A. The building of the castle of Monsalvat:

8. Amfortas. Von Wolzogen: Suffering Amfortas; Lavignac: Suffering.

As Parsifal, in Act III, touches Amfortas's wound with the Spear, and the wound closes, this theme recurs, with the augmented triad displaced from the melody to the accompanying chords, to sublime effect. That which had been steeped in suffering is now radiant with joy:

9. The prophecy, or pure-fool motif (*Torenspruch*):

9A is the mesmerizing sequence that occurs constantly throughout the work, influencing the harmonic and melodic context in which it occurs, and attracting to itself the evolving strains of Parsifal's struggle. 9B, the perfunctory closure, is heard only twice.

10. The riding motif:

This motif, associated with the wild ride of Kundry, develops in various ways throughout the work, being the harmonic basis for the magic spells in Klingsor's castle.

10A. Variants of the riding motif:

11. Kundry's scream:

Reduced to one or two octaves this motif places Kundry's existential angst in the narrative, sometimes merely as an exclamation mark, as here, during the bitter dialogue between Klingsor and Kundry:

12. Balsam/service. A motif associated with Kundry in her penitential aspect:

12A. A subsidiary motif accompanying Kundry's references to Arabia:

Several commentators emphasize the frequent use of rising and falling chromatic sequences in *Parsifal*, the first associated by Carl Dahlhaus and Derrick Everett with yearning, the second with suffering, as in the cry of woe, 25A. As I suggest below (motif 38), this association may be less significant than it seems. More important is the connection of the chromatic scale with the realm of magic, and of both with the mysterious Arabia that lies at the edge of the world.

13. Hero motif: or, Amfortas as hero:

14. The forest lake; the soothing influence of the lake. Everett calls this 'nature's healing':

A diminished and abridged form of this occurs later in Act I as Gurnemanz, reproaching Parsifal for shooting the swan, evokes the birds and beasts of the field as the boy's true companions, and again, in more pronounced form, in Act III, when Parsifal enters:

15. Sorcery, enchantment, the spell that binds Kundry:

15A recalls 12A: Arabia, enchantment. Important is the 'mystical' chord in the second bar, and its 'resolution' on the dominant major triad. The rising triad in the second bar is a contamination of the opening of 1 and 1A. See Chapter 5.

16. Sexual sorcery. Derived from 15 and 4, with an important enharmonic change:

This passage occurs twice, once when Gurnemanz describes Amfortas's falling for a seductress in Klingsor's domain, and once when Parsifal receives and escapes from Kundry's kiss.

17. The angelic bequest (variant of 3):

18. Klingsor:

The last two bars here derive from 15, by octave displacement.

19. Flower-maidens:

The first appearance of this, in 4/4 time, is when Gurnemanz describes to the squires the 'devilish beautiful women' in Klingsor's magic garden. In Act II the theme is adapted to a waltz rhythm (32), in a scene that shows the flower-maidens to considerable advantage, and far from devilish.

20. The Swan: a quotation from *Lohengrin*:

21. Parsifal. This fanfare introduces the unselfconscious hunter, and its naive horn-call harmonies convey a sense of good-hearted simplicity. Gradually, as the drama unfolds, the motif fragments, grows out in new directions, at last greeting Parsifal's return to the Grail temple in regal accents, emphasizing and multiplying the rhythmic figure in the fourth bar:

22. Herzeleide:

23. The question. Lorenz devotes a tortuous section to his claim that this sequence of two intervals is hidden in significant ways throughout the score:

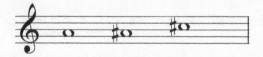

Wagner told King Ludwig that he had 'dispensed with the question' – in other words, that he had eliminated from his version of the story the idea that a question must be asked of Amfortas if he is to be healed of his wound. Instead he produced a far more suggestive narrative, in which the ruin of Monsalvat and the wound of its king can be healed only by the greatest self-sacrificing effort, involving an overcoming of the temptation that had ruined Amfortas. For Lorenz, however, the question is still there – it is too evocative an idea to be discarded; hence it must be hidden deep in the score.

24. The bells of the temple, and the call to the Eucharist.

A:

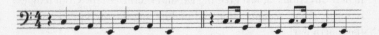

B:

25. Cries of woe (*Wehelaute*). Also *Heilandsklage*: the appeal of the Saviour. Those names are both used by von Wolzogen for a complex of motifs which lie at the heart of the drama, expressing the pain and lamentation which radiate from Amfortas to all those included in his fate. Lavignac calls the complex, with equal plausibility, 'l'appel au Sauveur' – the appeal *to* the Saviour, pointing to its appearance in the second act when Kundry cries out for inner refuge from the tyranny of Klingsor.

A (descending chromatic scale in parallel thirds):

B (melody loosely related to 5B and 6):

C (circle of fifths):

The combination of these three ideas, together with scalar and arpeggiated fragments from the repertoire of baroque 'affects', creates the image of a desolation beyond endurance, which bursts through the fabric of the score during the Act I transformation music, and is thereafter never far from the listener's consciousness.

26. Amfortas's lament. A melody given to Amfortas in his agony:

27. The invitation to communion. This is sung over the ostinato bass-line of the bells, 24A. The fourth bar of A is derived from 2, the Grail motif, the first two bars of B are derived from 3, the motif of faith:

A:

zum letz - ten lie - bes mah - le ge - rüst - et tag für Tag

B:

28. The love-feast (a kind of 'school song' version of 1):

29. Parsifal in Klingsor's castle.

A. The fool observed, variant of 9A:

B. The fight, derived from 10A:

30. Lament of the flower-maidens:

The five-note accompanying phrase here becomes the pleading motif **38A**, and permeates the entire scene between Parsifal and Kundry, reaching into Act III before wilting away.

31. Caresses of the flower-maidens:

32. Quarrelling flower-maidens:

33. Kundry's *berceuse*:

34. Love's sorrow, guilt:

33, 34 and 5 are brought beautifully together as Kundry coaxes Parsifal towards the kiss that is to turn both of them in a new direction.

35. Kundry's longing:

36. Kundry's torment:

Derived from 11, with a reminiscence of 26, this is taken to its extreme with Kundry's confession that she saw the Saviour in his agony and laughed.

37. Kundry's pleading, also called, following von Wolzogen, the 'devotion' motif (*Hingebende Motiv*). It is introduced with Kundry's plea: 'Laß mich an seinem Busen weinen':

38. Lamenting, pleading and yearning motifs. The first of these occurs as the flower-maidens lament the injuries of their paramours; it is prominent in the scene between Parsifal and Kundry, and also reappears at the end of the Act III Prelude and elsewhere in Act III; the second, which is a retrograde version of the first, is identified as a separate motif ('yearning') by Everett. In both cases the coincidence of the two voices at the central octave creates a harmonic hollowness, which is very much part of the *Parsifal* vision: not so much yearning as desolation. It seems to me quite wrong to identify 38B with the familiar 'desire' motif (*Sehnsuchtmotiv*) from *Tristan*, where it is absorbed into a network of voice-led chromatic harmony. The *Tristan* idiom avoids octave coincidences of this kind and treats the chromatic scale as the primary architectonic device.

A:

B:

(Kundry: 'Bist du Erlöser . . .')

The octave doubling of 38A is put to striking use at the end of Act II, when a series of stark dissonances associated with Kundry are moved towards an exhausted cadence in B minor, in which the octave G pushes towards a subdominant harmony:

39. Desolation. The futile journey and the passage of years (Lavignac calls this 'the desert'):

39A. Vestiges of desolation. The intervals of 39, rearranged, appear in another image of the Waste Land:

This accompanies a fragmented version of Parsifal's theme, as he appears in Act III, and also serves once or twice as a bass line to 9, the prophecy.

40. Straying, though associated by Kufferath with Kundry ('*Kundry vaincue, brisée*'). The motif can be heard as an extreme version of the Dresden Amen:

41. The resolved fool. A diminution of 9. The phrase B is identified by Everett as an independent motif; he calls it the 'waking' motif, since it is associated with Kundry's awakening from sleep in Acts II and III. Von Wolzogen calls it, more plausibly, the *Kampfruf*, the call to fight on:

However, the phrase also accompanies Parsifal's cry of woe when Kundry, in Act II, comes to the end of her narrative of Herzeleide's death:

Hence it should be acknowledged as an independent leitmotif.

42. The struggling fool. A variant of 41B, but with a bass-line recall-ing 15, and the dissonant harmony of Kundry's scream. The motif situates the fool among the temptations from which he has escaped:

43. The distress of Monsalvat (a reminiscence of 37). Lavignac describes this as the second form of the desert motif (39); von Wolz-ogen sees it as a shortened form of 39.

44. Consecration:

45. Purity. This motif comes to the fore in the consecration scene, and is subsequently attached to 48, the vision of the meadows on Good Friday.

46. Atonement:

This appears in the above harmonization near the beginning of Act III, when Gurnemanz refers to this holy day. Later, as Parsifal wonders at the blooming of the flowers in the meadow, the theme takes on a broader character:

47. Healing and holiness. References to the Spear and its healing virtues are linked in the opening of Act III to a motif in parallel fifths, as in the following two instances. The alto voice in the second example (in fact played an octave higher by violins in the orchestral score) is a variant of 9, the motif of the pure fool. The parallel fifths in the treble clef are a kind of distillation of the fool's successful journey, and appear several times in this connection. Of this passage Cosima records Wagner saying Gurnemanz 'howls for joy, and the fifths I've got there, you'll be amazed!' (*Diaries*, 21 December 1878):

Similar parallel fifths occur at the beginning of the act, when Gurnemanz notices the change in Kundry, and gives thanks for the holy day that has raised Kundry from sleep, as though ready to receive some holy blessing. Kufferath, noticing this, associates the following adaptation of 2 with sacredness generally, and remarks on the absence of any notes in common binding the chords of the first bar, a feature that recalls the *Stabat Mater* of Palestrina:

(In 1848 Wagner made an adaptation of Palestrina's *Stabat Mater*, which he edited and published in 1877.)

48. Good Friday meadows:

49. Innocence:

50. Obsequies. In the course of this extraordinary scene the solemn ostinato **A** grows to incorporate a variety of grim lamentations, of which **B** and **C** are typical, **C** being accompanied by the bells of the temple:

A:

B:

C:

51. Redemption. The *Grundthema* shortened and resolved, this first occurs when Gurnemanz expresses his joy on learning that the Spear has been retrieved:

52. Amfortas's despair. Certain phrases are repeated and embellished in Amfortas's final despairing monologue, and among them these two are prominent:

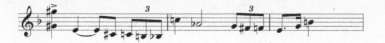

Both phrases take their shape from 8, the original theme of Amfortas's suffering.

53. Amfortas's prayer to Titurel. Von Wolzogen calls this the *Weihegrüß*, the reverential greeting. This recalls the rhythm of 17 and leads into it, but also conveys Amfortas's sense of being totally abandoned:

54. Amfortas's pleading. Close cousin of 34, which forges a connection between Parsifal's guilt towards his mother and Amfortas's guilt towards his father.

References

PREFACE

1 Friedrich Nietzsche, *The Case of Wagner* and *Nietzsche Contra Wagner*, tr. Thomas Common, London, 2013, p. 182.

2 See Robert Gutman, *Richard Wagner: The Man, His Mind and His Music*, London, Secker & Warburg, 1968; Mark A. Weiner, *Richard Wagner and the Anti-Semitic Imagination*, Lincoln, Nebr., University of Nebraska Press, 1995; Philippe Godefroid, *Richard Wagner, l'ecclésiaste anti-sémite*, Paris, L'Harmattan, 2011; Michael Steinberg, *The Trouble with Wagner*, London and Chicago, Chicago University Press, 2018.

3 For example, L. J. Rather, *Reading Wagner: A Study in the History of Ideas*, Baton Rouge, Louisiana State University Press, 1990, chs. 5 and 6.

I. THE QUEST

1 Lucy Beckett, *Richard Wagner: Parsifal*, Cambridge, Cambridge University Press, 1981.

2 Ulrike Kienzle, *. . . dass wissend würde die Welt: Philosophie und Religion in den Musikdramen Richard Wagners*, Würzburg, Verlag Königshausen und Neumann, 2005.

3 Joseph Campbell, *The Masks of God*, vol. IV, *Creative Mythology*, New York, Viking Press, 1970, pp. 405–570.

4 Friedrich Nietzsche, 'Nietzsche Contra Wagner', in *The Portable Nietzsche*, ed. Walter Kaufmann, New York, Viking Press, 1954, p. 675.

5 Richard Wagner, 'Religion and Art', in *Richard Wagner's Prose Works*, tr. William Ashton-Ellis, London, Kegan Paul, Trench, Trübner, 1897, vol. 6.

6 *Cosima Wagner's Diaries*, 2 vols., eds. M. Gregor-Dellin and D. Mack, London, Collins, 1978–80, vol. 2, entry for 20 September 1879.

7   See, e.g., Arthur Schopenhauer, *The World as Will and Representation*, tr. E. F. J. Payne, New York, Dover, 1969, vol. 2, ch. 17.

8   See esp. ibid., vol. 1, ch. 51.

9   The etymology of 'Munsalvaesche' points to 'Mont sauvage', wild castle, rather than 'Mons salvationis' or 'Mont de salut', castle of salvation. But there is an ambiguity here, and Wolfram plays with it, as does Wagner with the name 'Monsalvat'.

10 *Cosima Wagner's Diaries*, vol. 1, entry for 24 March 1877.

11 See Mircea Eliade, *The Sacred and the Profane*, tr. J. Tillard and R. Trask, New York, Harcourt, Brace, 1957, especially ch. 2, 'Sacred Time and Myths'.

12 Dieter Borchmeyer, *Das Theater Richard Wagners – Idee, Dichtung, Wirkung*, Stuttgart, P. Reclam, 1982. Erich Heller, *Disinherited Mind: Essays in Modern German Literature and Thought*, Harmondsworth, Penguin Books, 1952. Heller was referring specifically to the powerful religious sentiments expressed in Rilke's *Duino Elegies*.

13 See G. W. F. Hegel, *The Philosophy of Right*, tr. T. M. Knox, Oxford, Clarendon Press, 1952, para. 161. Hegel's thought mirrors Christ's saying that husband and wife become 'one flesh', which God has joined (Mark 10:5–9).

14 The phrase is Browning's, from his great poem 'A Toccata of Galuppi's'. The sevenths here are major and minor, diminished and half-diminished, in a sequence that illustrates a point later made by Schoenberg, namely that the diminished seventh is not, as Rameau thought, a chord without a single root, but rather a minor ninth whose root has been excised. The same is true of the half-diminished seventh, one inversion of which forms the Tristan chord: it can be treated as a major ninth without the root. I discuss these matters further in Chapter 5.

2. WAGNER'S TREATMENT OF THE STORY

1   Note that, under the patronage of Peter the Venerable, abbot of Cluny, the community of scholars in Toledo was given the task of translating the Koran into Latin, a task that was finished by the English monk Robert of Ketton in 1143. The half-century that saw the rise of the Grail literature thereafter saw a growing interest in the Muslim faith. See Alexander Bevilacqua, *The Republic of Arabic Letters*, Cambridge, Mass., Harvard University Press, 2018. See also P. Ponsoye, *Islam et le Graal*, Paris, Denoël, 1957.

2 For some of the many conjectures concerning the meaning of the term 'graal', and the origins of its religious significance in Druidic and other cults, see Maurice Kufferath, *Le Théatre de R. Wagner, de Tannhaeuser à Parsifal*, vol. 4, 2nd edn, Leipzig, 1893, ch. 1, '*Parsifal*'. Wagner himself accepted the now discredited story that the word derived from 'Saint Greal', a corruption of 'Sang Réal', the royal or real blood of the Saviour. See Richard Wagner, *The Diary of Richard Wagner 1865–1882* ('The Brown Book'), ed. Joachim Bergfeld, tr. George Bird, London, Cambridge University Press, 1980, p. 47.

3 Numbers refer to the list of leitmotifs in Chapter 6.

4 The title of a well-known and very relevant book by René Girard: *Des choses cachées depuis la fondation du monde*, tr. as *Things Hidden since the Foundation of the World*, tr. Stephen Bann and Michael Metteer, Stanford, Stanford University Press, 1987.

5 'Brown Book', p. 55.

6 Robin Holloway, 'Experiencing Music and Imagery in *Parsifal*', in *On Music: Essays and Diversions*, Brinkworth, Claridge Press, 2003, pp. 53–67.

7 Claude Lévi-Strauss, 'Ouverture' to *Le Cru et le cuit*, Paris, Plon, 1964.

8 René Girard, *La Violence et le sacré*, Paris, Grasset, 1972; Mary Douglas, *Purity and Danger: An Analysis of Concepts of Pollution and Taboo*, in *Collected Works*, vol. 2, London, Routledge, 2002.

9 Magic survived, of course, and religion remained intricately entwined with it. See Keith Thomas's witty exploration, *Religion and the Decline of Magic*, London, Allen Lane, 1971. Weber remarks somewhere that what defines a god, as opposed to the spirits conjured by the magician, is that a god cannot be coerced.

10 Douglas, *Purity and Danger*, ch. 6.

11 Wagner himself makes the connection with the Wandering Jew in his sketch of 1865. See 'Brown Book', p. 54. On the names of Kundry see the illuminating discussion in Anthony Winterbourne, *A Pagan Spoiled: Sex and Character in Wagner's Parsifal*, London, Associated University Presses, 2003, pp. 64–7.

12 Suggested by Johann Joseph von Görres (1776–1848), German writer and theologian, in his *Lohengrin, ein altdeutsches Gedicht* (1813). Arabic does not have any consonant corresponding to 'p', and in Persian 'fal parsi' denotes the horoscope.

13 Surely a reminiscence here of Heine, set by Schumann (Wagner's least favourite composer), 'Das Lied soll schauern und beben/Wie der Kuss von ihrem Mund . . .'

14 'Brown Book', p. 57.

15 For some of the contemporary reactions see Kufferath, *Théatre de R. Wagner*, pp. 213–21. For Stravinsky the climax of the work was 'unseemly and sacrilegious' (*An Autobiography*, New York, Simon and Schuster, 1956, p. 59), for Debussy (who regarded the score with the greatest reverence) it was merely 'ridiculous' ('Monsieur Croche the Dilettante Hater', tr. B. N. Langdon Davies, in *Three Classics in the Aesthetic of Music*, New York, Dover, 1962, pp. 46–9).

3. CONFRONTING THE ENIGMA

1 For an illuminating, and highly favourable, discussion of the Herheim production, see Mark Berry, *After Wagner: Histories of Modernist Music Drama, from Parsifal to Nono*, Woodbridge, The Boydell Press, 2014, ch. 7.

2 I am very grateful to Francis Maes for his unpublished paper discussing this and other productions, as attempts to reconfigure Wagner's idea of the sacred, and to make it accessible to modern audiences.

3 Theodor Adorno, *Versuch über Wagner*, 1952; tr. by Rodney Livingstone as *In Search of Wagner*, London, New Left Books, 1981.

4 That is the version of John 1:29 in the King James Bible and the Book of Common Prayer, which correctly translates the Greek αιρων. The Vulgate and the Tridentine mass address the Agnus Dei, 'qui *tollis* peccata mundi': i.e. who bears the burden of our sins. There is no implication that he *takes them away*.

5 The description of the Grail king as 'the Fisher King' has a complex rationale. The *roi pêcheur* who fishes is also the *roi pécheur* who sins, and in both Chrétien and Wolfram the Grail king enters the narrative as a fisherman, either actual or disguised. The symbolism of the fisherman as the one on whom rebirth depends has Christian as well as pagan antecedents. The matter is discussed in both Weston and Campbell – see the footnotes following.

6 J. Weston, *From Ritual to Romance: Folklore, Magic and the Holy Grail*, Cambridge, Cambridge University Press, 1920, p. 19.

7 Joseph Campbell, *The Masks of God*, vol. IV, *Creative Mythology*, New York, Viking Press, 1970, p. 459.

8 Emma Jung and Marie-Louise von Franz, *The Grail Legend*, Princeton, Princeton University Press, 1998.

9 Richard Wagner, *Opera and Drama*, in *Prose Works*, vol. 2, Lincoln, Nebr., University of Nebraska Press, 1994, Part 2, Section III.

10 Max Scheler, *Über Scham und Schamgefühl*, in *Schriften aus dem Nachlass*, I, Bern, Francke, 1957.

11 For the phenomenologists, see ibid.; Aurel Kolnai, *Sexual Ethics: The Meaning and Foundations of Sexual Morality*, tr. Francis Dunlop, Aldershot, Ashgate, 2005; Dietrich von Hildebrand, *In Defense of Purity* (1927), new edn, Steubenville, Oh., Hildebrand Press, 2017. See also Mary Douglas, *Purity and Danger: An Analysis of Concepts of Pollution and Taboo*, in *Collected Works*, vol. 2, London, Rouledge, 2002. The issue has been discussed, though in other terms, by Bernard Williams, *Shame and Necessity*, Berkeley, University of California Press, 1993.

12 On Shakespeare see Ewan Fernie, *Shame in Shakespeare*, London and New York, Routledge, 2002.

13 Letter to King Ludwig of 7 September 1865.

14 Jean-Paul Sartre, *Being and Nothingness*, tr. Hazel Barnes, London, Methuen, 1959.

15 Ibid., p. 398.

16 I am using the term 'intentionality' in the sense given to it by the phenomenologists, and notably by Edmund Husserl, to denote the general character of 'aboutness' that characterizes our states of mind.

17 Ibid., p. 375.

18 Eva Rieger, *Leuchtende Liebe, Lachender Tod*, Mannheim, Artemis Verlag, 2009, tr. by Chris Walton as *Richard Wagner's Women*, Woodbridge, The Boydell Press, 2011.

19 T. S. Eliot, 'Poetry and Belief', in *The Use of Poetry and the Use of Criticism*, Cambridge, Mass., Harvard University Press, 1933.

20 Rieger, *Leuchtende Liebe, Lachender Tod/Richard Wagner's Women*.

21 Friedrich Nietzsche, *The Case of Wagner*, section 9, in Nietzsche, *The Case of Wagner* and *Nietzsche Contra Wagner*, tr. Thomas Common, London, 2013.

22 In Thomas Mann, *Pro and Contra Wagner*, tr. Allan Blunden, ed. Erich Heller, London, Faber and Faber, 1985, p. 99.

23 Arthur Schopenhauer, *The World as Will and Representation*, tr. E. F. J. Payne, New York, Dover, 1969, vol. 1, p. 254.

4. SIN, LOVE AND REDEMPTION

1   *Cosima Wagner's Diaries*, 2 vols., eds. M. Gregor-Dellin and D. Mack, London, Collins, 1978–80, vol. 2, entry for 20 September 1879.

2   O. Strobel, ed., *König Ludwig II und Richard Wagner: Briefwechsel*, Karlsruhe, Braun Verlag, 1936–9, vol. 1, p. 82, quoted and translated in Lucy Beckett, *Parsifal*, Cambridge, Cambridge University Press, 1981, pp. 137–8.

3   It is worth noting, however, that there are ways of translating St Paul's theology of hope into the pursuit here and now of the 'Kingdom', so allowing a considerable amount of scepticism concerning the afterlife. The important voice here is that of Jürgen Moltmann, *Theology of Hope: On the Grounds and the Implications of a Christian Eschatology*, London, SCM Press, 1967. But it is clear that Wagner would have seen this move as merely another way of dramatizing the inner truth represented by Monsalvat, the truth of what we are in *this* world, here and now.

4   On the distinction here, and the connection of religious sacrifice to the ancient culture of gift-giving, see Moshe Halbertal, *On Sacrifice*, Princeton, Princeton University Press, 2012.

5   Sir James Frazer, *The Golden Bough*, especially the volumes on Attis and Adonis, summarized in the abridged edition, London, Macmillan, 1959, pp. 324–55; and Weston, *From Ritual to Romance*; Eliade, *Sacred and the Profane*.

6   René Girard, *La Violence et le sacré*, Paris, Grasset, 1976.

7   See René Girard, *Le Bouc émissaire*, Paris, Grasset, 1978.

8   'What is more harmful than any vice? Active pity for all the failures and all the weak: Christianity.' Friedrich Nietzsche, *The Anti-Christ*, in *The Portable Nietzsche*, ed. Walter Kaufmann, New York, Viking Press, 1954, p. 570.

9   See the illuminating article by David E. Cartwright, 'Schopenhauer's Compassion and Nietzsche's Pity', in *Schopenhauer-Jahrbuch* 69 (1988), pp. 557–67.

10 The key work here is Max Scheler's *Wesen und Formen der Sympathie*, 1913, tr. by Peter Heath as *The Nature of Sympathy*, London, Routledge and Kegan Paul, 1970. It is significant that Scheler avoids the term *Mitleid*, preferring the Greek *Sympathie* instead.

11 The philosophical basis for the idea of 'emotional knowledge' is given by Scheler, *Wesen und Formen der Sympathie*, and by Jean-Paul Sartre in his *Sketch for a Theory of the Emotions* (1939), tr. Philip Mairet, London, Methuen, 1962, emphasizing the elements of intentionality and valuation. The theme has been taken up in a series of works by Martha Nussbaum, including *Love's Knowledge*, Oxford, Oxford University Press, 1990, and *Upheavals of Thought: The Intelligence of*

Emotions, Cambridge, Cambridge University Press, 2001, ch. 7 of which contains an interesting discussion of compassion, and the Stoic suspicion of it as a form of weakness.

12 Edith Stein, *On the Problem of Empathy*, tr. Waltraut Stein, Washington DC, ICS Publications, 1989.

13 See R. Scruton, *The Soul of the World*, Princeton, Princeton University Press, 2014.

14 Verlaine's poem 'Parsifal', quoted in *The Waste Land*, belongs with a current of late Romantic and Symbolist literature inspired by *Parsifal*. See Stoddard Martin, *Wagner to "The Waste Land": A Study of the Relationship of Wagner to English Literature*, London, Macmillan, 1982.

15 On this point see the striking portrait of St Mark's Jesus given by John Carroll, *The Existential Jesus*, Melbourne, Scribe, 2007, and my commentary, 'John Carroll's Jesus', in Sara James, ed., *Metaphysical Sociology: On the Work of John Carroll*, London, Routledge, 2018.

16 Simon May, *Love: A History*, New Haven, Yale University Press, 2011.

17 Immanuel Kant, *Critique of Practical Reason*, 257, tr. T. K. Abbott, London, Longmans, Green, p. 311.

18 Søren Kierkegaard, *Works of Love*, tr. D. F. Swenson and L. M. Swenson, Princeton, Princeton University Press, 1960, p. 33.

19 Ibid., p. 48.

20 On which point there is no better commentary than Janáček's operatic transformation of Dostoevsky's *From the House of the Dead*.

21 Helen Prejean, *Dead Man Walking*, New York, Random House, 1993. The book was made into a moving and unusually successful opera by the librettist Terence McNally and composer Jake Heggie, premiered in 2000.

22 Max Scheler, *Vom Ewigen in Menschen*, vol. 1, *Religiöse Erneuerung*, Leipzig, Der Neue Geist Verlag, 1919.

23 Arthur Schopenhauer, *The World as Will and Representation*, tr. E. F. J. Payne, New York, Dover, 1969, vol. 1, p. 376.

24 A theme taken up by the Swedish Protestant theologian Anders Nygren, in his celebrated book *Agape and Eros* (1930, 1936), tr. Philip S. Watson, London, SPCK Press, 1953. For Nygren the transition from human *erōs* to divinely given *agapē* underlay the transition from the ancient to the Christian world.

25 C. S Lewis, *The Four Loves*, Glasgow, Geoffrey Bles, 1960, ch. 2.

26 Thomas Aquinas, *Summa Theologica*, 2a2ae, 23,1.

27 Schopenhauer, *World as Will and Representation*, vol. 1, p. 374.

28 *Cosima Wagner's Diaries*, vol. 2, p. 192.

29 Nussbaum, *Upheavals of Thought*, ch. 7.

30 Émile Durkheim, *Les Formes élémentaires de la vie religieuse*, 1912; tr. by J. W. Swain as *Elementary Forms of the Religious Life*, London, Allen and Unwin, 1926.

31 See also *Cosima Wagner's Diaries*, vol. 1, entry for 30 January 1877, in which Wagner is recorded as saying that it is the recovery of the Spear, not the question, that is the important thing.

32 I am obliquely referring here to the well-known attachment theory of John Bowlby.

5. THE MUSIC

1   *Cosima Wagner's Diaries*, 2 vols., eds. M. Gregor-Dellin and D. Mack, London, Collins, 1978–80, vol. 2, p. 216. The numbers that I assign to the thematic material are set out in the chapter that follows. Derrick Everett's catalogue of leitmotifs can be found on his Monsalvat website.

2   The Dresden Amen, composed by Johann Gottlieb Naumann (1741–1801) for use in the chapel royal in the Saxon capital of Dresden, would have been familiar to Wagner, both from his Dresden childhood and from his time as *Kapellmeister* in the chapel royal. It was used also by Mendelssohn in his Fifth ('Reformation') Symphony, and by other composers since. In *Parsifal* it is never a platitude but always something visionary, though I have met people who think that it occurs somewhat too often in the score.

3   Robin Holloway, 'Experiencing Music and Imagery in *Parsifal*', in *On Music: Essays and Diversions*, Brinkworth, Claridge Press, 2003, pp. 53–67.

4   See especially R. Cohn, 'Hexatonic Poles and the Uncanny in *Parsifal*', *The Opera Quarterly*, vol. 22, no. 2, 2007, pp. 230–48, and *Audacious Euphony*, Oxford, Oxford University Press, 2012, ch. 2.

5   See Cohn, 'Hexatonic Poles and the Uncanny in *Parsifal*', and *Audacious Euphony*, and David Lewin, 'Amfortas's Prayer to Titurel and the Role of D in *Parsifal*: The Tonal Spaces of the Drama and the Enharmonic Cb/D', in *Studies in Music with Text*, Oxford, Oxford University Press, 2009.

6   Alfred Lorenz, *Das Geheimnis der Form bei Richard Wagner*, vol. 4, *Parsifal*, Munich, Max Hesse's Verlag, 1933, reissued Tutzing, Hans Schneider, 1966.

7   Though both David Lewin and Richard Cohn make use of Lorenz's analysis in dividing up the score: see especially Lewin, 'Amfortas's Prayer to Titurel and the Role of D in *Parsifal*'.

8   Patrick McCreless, *Wagner's Siegfried: Its Drama, History and Music*, Ann Arbor, University of Michigan Research Press, 1982; Robert Bailey, ed., *Wagner: Prelude and Transfiguration from Tristan und Isolde* (Norton Critical Scores), New York and London, W. W. Norton, 1985; Reinhold Brinkmann, *Richard Wagner: Von der Oper zum Musikdrama*, Bern, Francke, 1978. See also Holloway, 'Experiencing Music and Imagery in *Parsifal*', in which Holloway shows the recurrence of melodic and harmonic structures through many of the leitmotifs in *Parsifal*.

9   Heinrich Schenker, *Free Composition*, tr. Ernst Oster, London, Longman, 1979.

10 See R. Scruton, *The Aesthetics of Music*, Oxford, Oxford University Press, 1947, pp. 313–29.

11 Carl Dahlhaus, *Richard Wagner's Music Dramas* (1971), tr. Mary Whitall, Cambridge, Cambridge University Press, 1979.

12 For a compelling account of one such period – Amfortas's desolate prayer to Titurel – see David Lewin, 'Amfortas's Prayer to Titurel and the Role of D in *Parsifal*'.

13 But see the discussion of the first movement of the Ninth Symphony in my *Understanding Music*, London, Bloomsbury, 2009, ch. 8.

14 See again Holloway, 'Experiencing Music and Imagery in *Parsifal*', pp. 53–67.

15 Ibid.

16 Ibid., pp. 55–6.

6. THE PRINCIPAL LEITMOTIFS

1   Hans von Wolzogen, *Thematic Guide through the Music of Parsifal*, New York, Schirmer, 1904; Albert Lavignac, *Le Voyage artistique à Bayreuth*, Paris, 1897; Maurice Kufferath, *Le Théatre de R. Wagner, de Tannhæuser à Parsifal*, vol. 4, *Parsifal*, 2nd edn, Leipzig, 1893.

Index

Musical motifs (leitmotifs) are numbered by the author in the text; these numbers are shown in the index in parentheses following the assigned name of a motif.

179